THE HEART AT THE HEART
OF THE WORLD

Ecology and Justice
An Orbis Series on Integral Ecology

The Orbis Series on Integral Ecology publishes books seeking to integrate an understanding of Earth's interconnected life systems with sustainable social, political, and economic systems that enhance the Earth community. Books in the series concentrate on ways to:

- reexamine human-Earth relations in light of contemporary cosmological and ecological science
- develop visions of common life marked by ecological integrity and social justice
- expand on the work of those exploring such fields as integral ecology, climate justice, Earth law, ecofeminism, and animal protection
- promote inclusive participatory strategies that enhance the struggle of Earth's poor and oppressed for ecological justice
- deepen appreciation for dialogue within and among religious traditions on issues of ecology and justice
- encourage spiritual discipline, social engagement, and the transformation of religion and society toward these ends

Viewing the present moment as a time for fresh creativity and inspired by the encyclical *Laudato Si'*, the series seeks authors who speak to ecojustice concerns and who bring into this dialogue perspectives from the Christian communities, from the world's religions, from secular and scientific circles, or from new paradigms of thought and action.

ECOLOGY & JUSTICE SERIES

THE HEART AT THE HEART OF THE WORLD

Re-visioning the Sacred Heart for the Ecozoic Era

Mary Frohlich

ORBIS BOOKS

Maryknoll, New York 10545

Founded in 1970, Orbis Books endeavors to publish works that enlighten the mind, nourish the spirit, and challenge the conscience. The publishing arm of the Maryknoll Fathers and Brothers, Orbis seeks to explore the global dimensions of the Christian faith and mission, to invite dialogue with diverse cultures and religious traditions, and to serve the cause of reconciliation and peace. The books published reflect the views of their authors and do not represent the official position of the Maryknoll Society. To learn more about Maryknoll and Orbis Books, please visit our website at www.orbisbooks.com.

Library of Congress Cataloging-in-Publication Data

Names: Frohlich, Mary, author.
Title: The heart at the heart of the world : re-visioning the sacred heart
   for the ecozoic era / Mary Frohlich.
Description: Maryknoll, NY : Orbis Books, [2024] | Series: Ecology and
   justice series | Includes bibliographical references and index. |
   Summary: "Reflection on the meaning of devotion to the Sacred Heart in
   light of ecological challenges"— Provided by publisher.
Identifiers: LCCN 2023044918 (print) | LCCN 2023044919 (ebook) | ISBN
   9781626985629 (print) | ISBN 9798888660201 (ebook)
Subjects: LCSH: Sacred Heart, Devotion to. | Sustainable
   development—Religious aspects—Catholic Church. | Human
   ecology—Religious aspects—Catholic Church.
Classification: LCC BX2158 .F764 2024 (print) | LCC BX2158 (ebook) | DDC
   232—dc23/eng/20231130
LC record available at https://lccn.loc.gov/2023044918
LC ebook record available at https://lccn.loc.gov/2023044919

CONTENTS

PART THREE: RE-VISIONING

INTRODUCTION

The Breakdown That Is Breaking Our Hearts

I grew up in South Dakota in the 1950s, in a family that was not religious or even "spiritual." We almost never attended church, and talk about God or any other religious theme was extremely rare. One day when I was about eight years old, we went for a family picnic at a small lake in the Black Hills. It was a pristine spot that few people knew about, but my father knew the way because he had grown up not far from there. The whole family went swimming in the lake. I paddled out about fifty feet, delighting in the cold water and the warm sunshine. Then something amazing happened. Even today I am almost tongue-tied in trying to say what it was. Since then I have had a long career as a theologian, a teacher of spirituality, and a nun, so I surely have many words that I can say. But if I am honest, I have to acknowledge that the original experience exceeded them all. The "heavens opened," so to speak, and the love at the heart of the world was revealed. I could not say any of that at the time. I only knew that the world—the actual, physical world, or "nature" as we call it—sparkled in its depths with a profundity and joy and mystery that I had never known anything about before.

So that is my first "heart story"—a personal story of being brought to the heart of things, without knowing where that was, what it meant, or where it would take me. Stories are the most basic way in which humans share meaning with one another. Orators and teachers know that the best way to get people's attention is to tell a story. Stories are key in every human being's urgent search to find a place of belonging in both fruitful social relationships and a sense of inner coherence. The more deeply we search, the more we find at the heart of our existence a mystery that can never be fully articulated—a timeless dwelling in God that is our source and our fathomless ground. Because we are creatures who live in time, however, we have a practical need for guiding models of how to navigate through the many challenges of life. It is in stories that we find—and generate—these models.

It is of the nature of stories, however, that they do not stand alone. No one has just one story. We always have many, because life's relationships and dramas are ineradicably multiple and complex. It is when we get stuck in the erroneous notion that there is just one story of "who I am" or "who we are" that we wreak the most misery upon ourselves and others. The story I told at the beginning of this Introduction is only one episode in "the story of my life." The epiphany at the lake was the beginning of a lifelong spiritual pilgrimage that has, to say the least, taken many twists and turns. I was sixty-two years old by the time I made final vows as a nun with the Society of the Sacred Heart. The pilgrimage continues, and this book is part of it. I want to put words not only on my experience but on what it revealed: that an infinite depth of love and life permeates all creation.

My personal pilgrimage has led me to articulate this in Christian terms, as the story of a living Heart at the very heart of the universe. I can never forget, however, that the essence of this story was shown to me long before I was baptized or had any religious language at all to name it. This truth is so far beyond language that it will inevitably generate many and diverse names—and stories. Or, to put it in the terms of my own tradition: Christ is not insulted by being given many names, or even no name at all, as long as we genuinely receive and live in the love of the Heart inscribed at the heart of creation.

Counterevidence: A heartless world?

It is not hard to find counterevidence for the claim that love is at the heart of creation. The world often seems like a truly heartless place. Going for a picnic and a swim in a mildly wild location may be fun for well-fed denizens of advanced technological societies, but those who have to make a living from the natural world know that it is often a hard, dangerous, fickle place for human beings. For the billions of poor all around the globe who depend on the rhythms of land, sky, and sea for survival, the combination of rampant resource over-exploitation plus climate change is increasingly making life almost impossibly difficult. Yet any effort on their part to migrate to wealthier areas of the world is met heartlessly with rejection or with consignment to camps where conditions often approximate torture.

In the modern technologized world, heartlessness often appears in the form of the unrelenting grind of impersonal structures or, even worse, the intrusion of senseless violence. An epidemic of loneliness, isolation, distrust, and anxiety is raging through contemporary societies. The causes are surely complex, but one significant contributing element is that a literal form of heartlessness is still enshrined in predominant modern intellectual traditions. Since the so-called European Enlightenment of the seventeenth century, we in the West have been taught that the physical world is basically nothing more than an inert resource to be exploited relentlessly for human benefit. Even living beings other than humans—and, too often, human beings other than white Europeans and Americans—have been similarly characterized. This modern dualism perniciously separates us from vital, sustaining connection with the Earth and its ecosystemic web of living creatures.

Influenced by this context, Christian theology and spirituality in the modern era (i.e., the seventeenth to early twentieth centuries) incorporated a similar mentality. Humans were regarded as the only creatures with "souls" and thus the only ones eligible for salvation. Our life on Earth is only a preparation or backdrop to our true destiny in heaven, which is "elsewhere." The main obstacle to arrival in heaven is the horror of sin, which primarily offends God, although it also has irreparably shredded the fabric of human relationships. Even though there is usually lip service to the biblical tradition that God originally created the world to be "good," this does little to counteract the sense that Earth itself is, indeed, a heartless place.

Yet persistent human traditions see things otherwise. Across numerous cultures and religions, many have proclaimed that, despite whatever cruel circumstances we may encounter, the core of creation is actually permeated by tenderness, compassion, and mutuality. To express this, the metaphor of the "heart" appears over and over again in spiritual traditions. The Mayan people of Mesoamerica, for example, always begin their invocations, "Oh great Heart of the Universe!" In her book *Heart*, Gail Godwin chronicles stories of the heart among the Sumerians, Egyptians, Hebrews, Hindus, Buddhists, Chinese, Japanese, and Greeks.[1] The present

---

1. Gail Godwin, *Heart: A Personal Journey through Its Myths and Meanings* (London: Bloomsbury, 2004), 22–79.

book focuses primarily on heart traditions within Christianity. Its thesis is that our Christian heart traditions can be a powerful resource for regenerating the vital flow of life within the web of human and more-than-human life on Earth.

An explanatory note on the expression "more-than-human" is in order here, since some readers may not be familiar with this phrase. In the literature on the ecological crisis and on the need for humans to reconnect with our Earth roots, this has become the standard term for referring to the complex ecological web of life, land, air, and water within which human life emerges and is sustained. It can also be used on a more localized scale for any part of this web with which someone is in relationship; for example, one might say: "The indigenous hunter had exquisite sensitivity to the sounds of the more-than-human world around him." Sarah Elton provides a more technical definition: "More-than-human refers to contexts in which multiple species and processes come together to produce a result."[2]

The first time I heard the term, I reacted against it because I thought it sounded almost like a deification of the natural world. I have learned, however, that this term was chosen in preference to "other-than-human" because the latter sets humans apart from the rest of the world and makes us the defining element. More-than-human does not define a hierarchy, but rather puts us in our place as completely interdependent with a far larger matrix of beings and elements. It tells the truth of our radical vulnerability in relation to the Earth and its processes.

---

2. Sarah Elton, "More-than-Human," in *Showing Theory to Know Theory: Understanding Social Science Concepts through Illustrative Vignettes*, ed. Patricia Ballamingie and David Szanto, vol. 1 (Ottawa, ON: Showing Theory Press, 2022), https://ecampusontario.pressbooks.pub/showingtheory/chapter/more-than-human/.

If the ancient heart traditions are to serve the vital needs of the twenty-first century, they will need to be substantially reworked. That will be the project of the remaining chapters of the book. Before we can begin again, however, we must first acknowledge how deeply our hearts are broken by our disconnection from the deep rhythms of life.

The breakdown that is breaking our hearts

In our time, the entire global community of life is collectively undergoing a traumatizing calamity. The unfolding ecological catastrophe that is manifested in—among other things—the ever-intensifying heat waves, fires, floods, and hurricanes of climate change; the daily news of the extinction of more species; the plastic and chemical pollution that extends both to the deepest oceans and to the blood of newborns; and the literal bulldozing of ecosystem after ecosystem, is far more than just one more difficult period in human history. Andy Fisher, who has developed an ecopsychology of widening our social fields until we are able to live the fullness of our ecological and cosmic kinship, calls the ecological crisis "both a spiritual crisis and a pathological disturbance in this largest of social fields."[3] It is so drastic that it could, in fact, be the end of human history.

Geologists say that the Cenozoic era, which lasted for 66 million years and saw the proliferation of life on Earth into 8.7 million species of plants and animals, as well as up to one trillion species of microorganisms, is coming to an end. Geological eras are divided into periods and epochs, and the final epoch of the Cenozoic is called the Holocene. Lasting 11,650

---

3. Andy Fisher, *Radical Ecopsychology: Psychology in the Service of Life*, 2nd ed, SUNY Series in Radical Social and Political Theory (Albany: State University of New York Press, 2013), 126.

years, this has been a time of mild climate that provided ideal conditions for humanity's flourishing. As it crashes to a close, what comes next is up for debate. Thomas Berry (1914–2009), a Passionist priest who clearly foresaw the ecological and spiritual implications of humanity's disconnection from the Earth, proposed that if humanity is to survive, the coming era must be the Ecozoic. By this he meant a time when human beings relearn how to live sustainably within the reality of our physical and spiritual interdependence with the Earth.[4]

Meanwhile, many in the scientific and philosophical communities have named the emerging geological epoch the Anthropocene, as a stark indication that every aspect of Earth's functioning—from air flow and ocean currents, to the chemical composition of soil and water, to which species survive and which die out—is now being shaped by human activity. Some of them regard that scenario positively, as if human technology were on the verge of truly mastering the Earth and making a better life for the human species. A more likely possibility, however, is that the changes humans have introduced will so radically undo the ecological balances upon which human life depends that the result will be the downfall of the human species. Even if total extinction is not the end result, the probability is high that in the not-very-distant future, all human societies will undergo extreme levels of chaos, violence, and death due to the effects of the deteriorating global ecosystem.

Even if we try to regard such a catastrophe as an event external to us, like, say, a tornado that devastates a nearby town where we have frequently walked and enjoyed life with our friends, such a scenario evokes a shiver in our hearts. The

---

4. Thomas Berry, *Thomas Berry: Selected Writings on the Earth Community*, ed. Mary Evelyn Tucker and John Grim, Modern Spiritual Masters (Maryknoll, NY: Orbis Books, 2014), 134–44.

problem with the attempt to ignore it is that this already-in-motion catastrophe is not external to us. We are the Earth. Even when we are not fully cognizant of it, the Earth means everything to us. At a primal level, the Earth is the motherly body within which our bodies take shape, and all the other Earth creatures are not only our companions but a support system without which we cannot survive. Experiencing the deterioration of the Earth is like living through the descent of a once-functioning family into toxicity, addictions, violence, and disease. Yet it is even more than that. Perhaps the most apt analogy is the experience of the people of Paradise, California, who in 2018 watched their beloved town and surrounding forests go up in flames. While many of us have not yet seen the flames of Earth's demise, we live in the dread of knowing they are just over the hill and headed this way.

The breakdown of the Earth is breaking our hearts. I will tell a small story of my own about this. When I lived in Chicago, I devoted many hours of labor to our backyard garden, to try to make it as friendly as possible to native wildlife. Sometimes I would sit in the far back section of the garden, just watching to see who or what would appear. One day I saw, for the first time in my life, a hummingbird moth. This is a moth that is as large as a small hummingbird and hovers in a similar manner. Although the books say they are not terribly rare, they are not often seen. My heart was moved with tender delight in the intricate beauty of the creature, and with joy that my efforts had made it possible for such a wondrous being to thrive in that place. Yet in the same movement of the heart, I also felt poignant sorrow. Although my labors had given this creature a livable niche for the time being, I felt the inevitability of its destruction already bearing down upon it. Even as I loved and delighted in the moth, my heart was broken by awareness of the looming threat to its entire web of life connections.

This was, obviously, not a response on a rational level. I did not actually know at that time whether hummingbird moths, specifically, are imminently in danger of extinction. Perhaps they will be able to survive, even if humans and many other species do go extinct. My response was a response of a heart that knows these are death-dealing times for all my kin, human and more-than-human. In these times, to open one's heart to the Earth community from which we come, or to any of its members, is to open oneself to a sorrow unto death.

Chaos, restitution, or quest?

The heart breaks when something or someone in whom one has deeply invested betrays, or is betrayed, in a profoundly disturbing manner. The energizing narrative moving toward an envisioned bright future that one was happily spinning is shattered, leaving one in agonizing confusion and chaos. The classic example is the romantic breakup: a person falls in love, invests many hopes and dreams in the relationship, and then is shockingly abandoned. But there are many other ways for the heart to break. In his book *The Wounded Storyteller,* Arthur Frank writes of how life-threatening illness affects the stories people tell about their lives.[5] The story-map that the ill person had been following with much vibrant energy suddenly seems to have landed on the trash heap, stinking and disintegrating before their very eyes. Much that Frank says about the impact of illness is relevant to other kinds of heartbreak as well, including our heartbreak over the fate of the Earth and its creatures.

Frank says that when faced with the shattering impact of a serious illness, the story-making imagination goes into overdrive

5. Arthur W. Frank, *The Wounded Storyteller: Body, Illness, and Ethics* (Chicago: University of Chicago Press, 1997).

to try to rebuild a viable story for oneself and one's witnesses. An early manifestation of this is what he calls the "naming story." The person feels an urgent need to find a name—in the case of illness, a diagnosis—for what has gone wrong. Under the circumstances of modern medicine, the naming story is often quickly followed by the "restitution narrative." This is a story about how life will soon return to normal, exactly the same as before. The hero of the restitution narrative is typically the doctor, the medical institution, or the healing regime that can restore one to health. If the cure is successful, such a person may resume their former self-story, without feeling much need for significant change. As we collectively face the current ecological crisis, we hear many restitution narratives about how technology will soon save us from any need to change our lifestyle.

Despite these efforts, many seriously ill people find themselves instead overcome by what Frank calls the "chaos narrative." A fully chaotic narrative has no plot; awful things just happen, one after another, and nothing comes of it. There is no sense of purpose, direction, or hope. Such a story is deeply anxiety-producing for listeners, who often try to steer the speaker towards a different story—whether it be the restitution narrative, or the silver lining ("there's always some good that comes out of bad things"), or the "count your blessings" story. The person who is truly experiencing chaos, however, will have none of it.

Not long ago a story appeared in the *Boston Globe* and other news outlets about William Good, a thirty-one-year-old man who became a paraplegic when his head hit the headrest during the crash of an Uber vehicle in which he was a passenger.[6] The story was mainly about Good's lawsuit against Uber

---

6. Tonya Alanez, "Uber Passenger Paralyzed in Crash Sues Company

for hiring the driver, who had other crashes on his record. As I read through the story, I began to feel uneasy. I realized at that point that I had an unconscious expectation that, as in so many news stories about tragic events, the focus would eventually arrive at how the victim was heroically overcoming his difficulties and making a new life despite his limitations. That type of news story sometimes even includes a line about how the victim realizes that they are actually a better person now because of all they suffered and overcame. All of us love such feel-good stories. It is as if we say to ourselves, "Yes, this is how I would respond if something terrible happened to me!"

Storytellers, including news outlets, typically prefer to tell the kind of stories that people enjoy hearing. They will often base a story on the smallest glimmer of hope or heroism, rather than tell an outright chaos narrative. In the case of William Good, they focused their story around the lawsuit in which he seeks financial compensation for his injuries. Perhaps one can interpret this as a kind of heroic resistance to his circumstances. Between the lines, however, it is easy to see that William Good is not telling any kind of feel-good or heroic story. His story is about how, in a single totally unexpected moment, he forever lost all possibility of access to everything he had loved and taken for granted—his bodily independence, his favorite pursuits, and his hoped-for future endeavors. The mood of his testimony was of heartbreak, depression, and anger, without any hint of a happy ending or a silver lining. Good's story is a chaos narrative. It made me uneasy because, on the level of story, it is one I instinctively resist having become my own.

---

for $63 Million," *Boston Globe*, January 25, 2022, https://www.bostonglobe.com/2022/01/25/metro/uber-passenger-paralyzed-crash-sues-company-63-million/.

The whole planet now seems to be living in the midst of the ultimate chaos narrative: one horrifyingly destructive event after another, going nowhere except over the precipice of the end of the world. It is not surprising that many close themselves off from this sorrow, since living in narrative chaos is the worst of all possible fates for a human being. A person can bear remarkably heavy loads of pain and loss if they can place their agony within a story of meaning. Viktor Frankl famously wrote about how people were able to survive the monstrous conditions of the German concentration camps if they could cling to a story of purpose or of love.[7] Those who had no such story, or who discovered that their version could not bear the strain of prolonged and dehumanizing suffering, usually fell into madness, deathly depression, or self-centered violence. Most of these did not live long.

Some try to sweeten the ecological chaos narrative by attributing it to God, who (it is said) will use the occasion to lift the elect above it into a different place called heaven. Another large cohort of human beings simply live in denial that any of this is happening. This is partly because they are busy and distracted by more immediate concerns, but it is also because it is too painful and frightening even to allow thoughts of such chaos and death into a corner of consciousness. Even more common is a version of Frank's "restitution narrative."[8] This is the optimistic assumption that, although we do indeed have a problem on our hands, it won't be long before humans find the way to fix the global ecosystem so we can all go back to happily enjoying our high-consumption lifestyles as usual. Finally, there are an increasing number who, like those whom Viktor

---

7. Viktor E. Frankl, *Man's Search for Meaning* (Boston: Beacon Press, 2006).

8. Frank, *The Wounded Storyteller.*

Frankl described as having lost all hope of finding meaning in their ordeal, fall into self-centered cynicism as a way of life.

Perhaps we cannot avoid a certain degree of grasping for some version of the ecological restitution narrative, for otherwise it is difficult to maintain our sanity. Frank proposes, however, another option: the "quest narrative." For people enduring severe illness, this is a story about the illness as a "hero's journey" in which the suffering and multiple unpredictable crises of illness are an initiation into wisdom, which can then be offered to others who are just setting out on their own quests. Such a story is not necessarily about being cured or recovering from the illness; it is about living fully and generatively through the process, even if the physical end point is disability or death. Applying this to the case of our planetary calamity, we look for stories that assist us in growing into people of wisdom even as we live in the midst of wounded ecosystems and care for dying species. An example of this approach is Meg Wheatley's training program for "Warriors for the Human Spirit," which seeks to prepare leaders who guide with generosity, insight, and compassion even under the current conditions of breakdown.[9]

Toward a new story

Frank observes that one of the characteristics of story-making is that it is an inherently relational activity. Even when I am only telling my story interiorly, it is an attempt to find the sense and direction of my life in terms that are both truthful to myself and meaningful to those with whom my life is intertwined.

---

9. Margaret J. Wheatley, "Warriors for the Human Spirit: Training To Be the Presence of Insight and Compassion," https://margaretwheatley.com/2020-europe-warriors-for-the-human-spirit-training/#top.

Every self-story is a testimony, a witness to the creative act of articulating the meaningfulness of a life. We incorporate and model ourselves on the stories we hear from those with whom we share life. When we can identify with the stories those around us tell, we feel a sense of community with them.

When we find no resonance with the stories that are affirmed in a community or institution, however, the vitality goes out of our participation and it is likely that we will soon drift away. This is one significant element of the accelerating drift away from churches and from participation in institutionalized religion. Living in a profoundly different world, people have great difficulty identifying with many of the "old" religious stories. Especially as this generation and the coming ones face the chaos inherent in ecological crisis, we have a profound need for a renovation—or, as I like to call it, a "re-visioning"— of our religious stories. We need stories that can help us to become people of wisdom who are not only able to navigate in such turbulent times, but can also build supportive, healthy communities inclusive of the human and more-than-human worlds.

William Thompson-Uberuaga has written that the best Christology (the theology explaining the identity and role of Jesus Christ) is done in stories generated by personal experience of participating in Christ's life.[10] Based in my own experience as well as that of a burgeoning number of others who offer similar testimony, this book offers a story of the Heart of God as literally the heart of all creation. The cosmic Heart dwells in every created being—including those that are regarded as inanimate in the modern mentality. Our spirituality and theology will be transformed by embracing the "new animism" that regards every being (including humans) as a node in webs of living relationality, rather than as lonely, heartless, and hierar-

---

10. William Thompson-Uberuaga, *Christology and Spirituality* (New York: Crossroad, 1991).

chically arranged individuals. While this book is by no means a systematic Christology, one of its goals is to refresh and update our participative understanding of what it means to discover the Heart at the heart of the world.

A friend who read my book proposal commented that this is not a completely new story, since similar stories can be found in some ancient Christian traditions—not to mention among indigenous peoples and in various other religions and cultures. The truth is that all our stories come to birth in a process something like that of a jazz musician, who riffs on old tunes while reaching creatively for new ones. No one creates a story *ex nihilo* (from nothing); we always have old stories (sometimes several of them) playing in the back of our heads as we reach to tell a new story that will be fresh and compelling for our hearers. The reader will no doubt hear the melodies of many old stories playing in the background of this new story.

Not all who awaken to this Heart will join our Christian churches, nor will they necessarily use the kind of Christian theological language that I am using here. Many who do not call themselves Christians may be more attuned to the call of the incarnate God than are many baptized, churchgoing Christians. Living heartfully in everyday life, humbly risking goodness, actively respecting every living creature and ecosystem, going all in to assist movements for peace, justice, and the integrity of creation—this is what it means to live in tune with the Heart at the heart of the world.

Overview of the book

After this Introduction, the book is organized in three parts. Part One, "Heart Devotion," includes a chapter exploring the meaning of heart and heartfulness, and a second chapter providing a brief historical survey of Christian devotion to the Heart of Jesus. Part Two, "In the Heart of the World," offers the main development of the theme. Three chapters explore the implications of Christian animism, a Heart-focused evolutionary Christology, and the wildness and queerness of God's kindom. Three more chapters delve into how Christ may "person" in any part of creation, wisdom as participation in the depths of created being, and the Eucharist as interspecies gift economy. Finally, Part Three summarizes a "re-visioning" of the Sacred Heart in terms of the accompaniment of the Pierced Heart. The final chapter develops the idea of "reparation in the key of accompaniment."

Concluding comments

During more than thirty-five years of being a student and then a professor in higher education, I got used to writing for academics. That kind of writing has to be very precise and heavy with footnotes. This book is different. It still has some footnotes—I can't help it after all these years, and besides that, I hope someone may actually want to follow up on some of the ideas presented here! My goal in this book, however, is to write an evocative and inspiring text for a wide range of readers. In dealing with theological issues and with biblical texts, I have given myself the freedom to reflect creatively rather than to develop each insight in the thorough, nuanced manner of a scholarly essay.

I love scholarship with all its plodding detail and carefully worked out thought processes, and I am far from being ready to renounce that work completely. At this stage in my life and in the life of planet Earth, however, I find that communicating a vision that could possibly make a difference feels more urgent than taking the years (or decades) it would require to work it all out with full scholarly precision. In tune with this book's themes, I have written from my heart. It would be a

bonus if some of the book's readers went on to explore these issues themselves, perhaps eventually writing something far better on these themes than what I have been able to produce.

One other prefatory comment may be in order, in view of
current sensitivities in regard to cultural appropriation. At various times in this book, I refer to indigenous peoples and indigenous ways of thinking. In some cases I quote indigenous
writers, while in other places my comments are more general.
I myself am not indigenous, nor do I have a personal relationship with any specific indigenous community. I am not under
the illusion that white "settlers" such as myself have the ability
or the right to claim indigenous culture for ourselves. Nor do I
believe that anyone, settler or indigenous, will be able to go
back to the way life was in earlier times; we all have to go forward together with what is given to us now. As we do that, I believe that we who are not indigenous can and must learn as
much as we can from those who have centuries of experience
in living more wisely on the land than our own people have.

In his book *Think Indigenous*, Lakota teacher Doug Good
Feather makes a similar point as he writes: "There's a fine line
between the appreciation of a culture and the appropriation of
a culture."[11] He defines appropriation as claiming the language,
symbols, rituals, and so on of an indigenous culture as one's
own, which is a form of stealing. Appreciating the culture, on
the other hand, can include recognizing and amplifying the
wisdom of that culture's spiritual teachings as a positive and
needed force in our world today. I hope I have respectfully
stayed on the correct side of this fine line that Good Feather
and others have drawn.

---

11. Doug Good Feather, *Think Indigenous: Native American Spirituality for a Modern World* (Carlsbad, CA: Hay House, 2021), 6.

PART ONE

HEART DEVOTION

1

Vulnerability and Heartfulness

Years ago, I remember being puzzled when a friend asked, "How's your heart?" I knew she was not asking about my physical heart. I was pretty sure she was also not asking for the usual long-winded recounting of my ongoing struggles and complaints and hopes. She was asking something subtler—something more foundational and person-defining. I intuited that appropriate answers might be phrases like "at peace," "sorrowful," "troubled," or "full of joy." I couldn't answer her question that day. I probably mumbled something noncommittal about "doing OK."

Only much later did I learn to diagnose my lack of ability to feel, or even identify, the place of the heart. The truthful answer to her question would have been, "hurting." But saying that would have opened the door either to being asked for a much longer and more intimate recounting or to the retraumatizing experience of having one's pain unheard. It was simpler to just not feel it in the first place.

I tell this story, not to exaggerate the uniqueness of my hurting heart, but just the opposite. Hurting, broken, traumatized hearts are everywhere, and often one of their chief strategies is to do everything in their power to prevent anyone—even themselves—from knowing it. Without downplaying the fact that the causes and degrees of brokenness of heart vary widely, there is a sense in which all of us have broken hearts. It is this brokenness that motivates both our worst, most destructive behavior and our best, most creative pursuits. We all have broken hearts because the heart is the locale of greatest relationality, and therefore of greatest vulnerability.

The place of the heart

Before exploring more deeply the vulnerability of the heart, we first must ask what it means to speak of "the place of the heart." We begin with the physical heart, an organ just off-center in the chest, that unceasingly pumps life-giving blood throughout the body. The rhythm of this organ accompanies us everywhere from a few weeks after conception to death, adjusting to a faster pace with exercise or intense emotion and to a slower pace with relaxation and sedentary activities. A great deal of scientific research is currently being done on the nerve connections among the brain, heart, and gut, giving much insight into how emotional and physiological reactions resonate among all three.[1] "Heart trouble" (like "gut trouble") is a body-mind-spirit condition that is not always initiated purely in the physical dimension.

My friend's question, though, pointed to another meaning of "heart." We identify our heart as the center of deep, affective connection with our own aliveness as well as with people, communities, places, and whatever else we love. The heart is where we feel moved by love, compassion, intimacy, and joy—as well as by sorrow, anguish, or shock. It is with the heart that we in-

---

1. Rollin McCraty, *Science of the Heart: Exploring the Role of the Heart in Human Performance*, vol. 2 (Boulder Creek, CO: Heartmath, 2015).

vest our trust and our care in others. The heart is the place of courage (a word derived from *cor,* Latin for "heart"), conviction, and deep choice. It is the core from which we claim our moral character—our personal willingness to stand for what we believe to be right, even in the face of loss and opposition. These are the qualities of living "heartfully."

Those who pursue the spiritual life take all this to a yet deeper level. The Desert Fathers and Mothers (4th–6th c. CE) considered the heart the primary organ of prayer. St. Augustine famously said, "Our hearts are restless until they rest in God." St. Teresa of Avila repeatedly referred to the heart as the place where she knew God's presence.[2] Perhaps the most famous story about this is her recounting of a vision of her heart being pierced by a spear wielded by a cherub. Bernini's statue of Teresa swooning in erotic ecstasy is the best-known interpretation of this experience. Another way to interpret it, though, is that it is an imagistic way of expressing the experience of an intimacy so tender, and so beyond one's capacity to encompass it, that it hurts. Such is the touch of God in one's heart.

Although all these meanings of "heart" name an interiority, they also necessarily point through that to the exteriority of multiple relationships. Every experience of touch or intimacy is situated historically as well as geographically, physically, culturally, interpersonally, and more. The heart has its own ecology, in the most literal sense: it exists in, and only in, a dynamic web of relations that interweave a vast variety of actors. This book aims to spell out some of what it means to live in the vulnerable heart of that web.

---

2. Joseph F. Chorpenning, "Heart Imagery in Santa Teresa," in *Studies in Honor of Elias Rivers* (Digitalia, Inc., 1989), 49–58, http://ezproxy.ctu.edu:2048/login?url=http://search.ebscohost.com/login.aspx?direct=true&db=hlh&AN=32060654&scope=site.

Vulnerability

We are subject to having our hearts broken because we are intrinsically vulnerable creatures. We are born completely enmeshed in bodily and emotional relationship with everything we encounter. Only gradually do we begin to sort out what to focus on, whom to invest with our attachment, and how to assert and defend ourselves in an overwhelming world. Yet no matter how strong and autonomous we become, we never leave behind the fundamental reality that we are creatures enmeshed in relationships, and to be in relationship is to be vulnerable. In this book, we focus not only on interpersonal and social relations with other humans but also and even more importantly on our multifaceted relations with the entirety of the more-than-human world.

In modern Western culture, acknowledging vulnerability is countercultural. Rather than being viewed as the positive quality of tender openness, it is frequently eschewed as a contemptible form of weakness. Yet fundamentally, we are vulnerable because we are interdependent, and interdependence is the ground of the potential richness of life just as much as it opens us to being wounded. In this book we will be exploring both dimensions. Our main focus will be on the joy, delight, and fullness of life that we can discover when we regain the felt sense of living participation in the networks of the more-than-human world. It would be culpably Pollyannaish, however, to stop there. Anyone who is tuned in to even a small part of the web of life on Earth feels almost overwhelming grief at seeing how much life and beauty are being irretrievably lost due to the irresponsibility of human action. In our time, to open ourselves to the more-than-human world is to open ourselves to sorrow. Yet, as we will see, that is not a reason to remain in denial; it is, rather, a call to live even more fully from the vulnerability and tenderness of the heart.

Four functions of the heart

A close analysis suggests that the heart (in the more-than-physical sense) has at least four essential functions in human life, which can be termed interiority, bonding, belonging, and meaning. First, the interiority of the heart is the sense of a safe, stable, and secret interior space to which one can retreat for reflection, rest, and prayer. This is the heart as a space of a solitude that is not lonely, but rather, refreshing and grounding. Profound depths of holy presence and joy may be discovered in the awareness of the heart. Feeling safe to enter and explore the interiority of one's heart, however, generally depends on feeling a degree of safety in the other dimensions of heart experience.

The bonding heart is eager to find others who are worthy of being welcomed in for long-term, tender, trusting relationships. We speak of this when we say, "you are in my heart" or "I hold you in my heart." This is the heart as the place of love and friendship. When one person allows another into their heart, the two become emotionally and psychologically interdependent. The deeper the bond of the heart, the more this is the case. To lose a person or other creature with whom one has such a heart-bond, whether through absence, death, or betrayal, feels like losing an essential part of oneself.

The heart seeking belonging wants to connect and care on a broader basis, reaching outward to give and receive in networks of relationship. This is the heart knowing itself as caring and being cared for through committed participation in extended family, community, associations, political parties, church, nation, or local bioregion. Here the heart-relationships are more diffuse and less intense, but equally essential to one's well-being.

Loss or betrayal on this level is also devastating, although the heart's investment in a network gives it more options for finding a refuge than when the investment is in a single relationship.

Finally, the heart as locale of meaning seeks a way to actively invest itself in making the world a better place. For some this "world" that they hope to affect may be as small as their own home or back yard, while for others it may literally be the whole globe. For some it may be focused within a secular career, while for others it may lead to action for social justice or to commitment to a religious vocation. In any of these cases, the investment of the heart means that the person is willing to put their best thought, creativity, and work into making the project a success. If the person "loses heart" for the project, however, this investment will wane, and such work will become only a burdensome chore.

In real life, of course, these four dimensions of heart are more often than not intertwined with one another in complex ways. A good marriage, for example, is not only a tender one-on-one bond but also respects solitude, mediates various forms of belonging, and supports each one's investment in meaningful projects. One of the significant sources of problems in marriage is a lack of appropriate balance among these four. A marriage commitment means giving a central priority to the pair bond, so a partner overly devoted to solitude, to group activities apart from their spouse, or to work can lead to problems. On the other hand, a tyrannous demand that the life of the couple trump everything else in their lives is also a recipe for unrest. The heart needs its own inner space, its special relationships, its participatory belonging, and its meaningful projects; without all of these, it will not be fulfilled.

Even though all these qualities and capacities of "heart" clearly go beyond simple physicality, talk about the heart and heartfulness remains grounded in that embodied organ that beats out the rhythm of every moment of life. Many people instinctively place a hand over the heart when they are deeply moved by something; the depth of feeling seems to emanate from that physical area. Heart is an embodied reality—or perhaps better said, it is a whole-person reality. When we say, "This comes from my heart," we mean that it comes from the depth and truth and wholeness of our embodied spirit.

In recent years the term "heartfulness" has emerged to express the potential of the heart's deep embodied presence. This is Robert Sardello's summary from his book *Heartfulness*:

> Heart awareness, heartfulness, locates being fully human within the soul and spiritual center of the body, the heart. Practices of heartfulness contemplatively engage the actual organ of the heart, inwardly revealing what it is like to be incarnated in body and world. In developing the capacity to creatively radiate from the center outward, the holy, whole, nature of the human body reveals itself as intimately united with imagination, creative presence, Earth-unity, and the unfolding of the livingness of all things. It feels like our natural state, forgotten long ago.[3]

In this book we explore the implications of heartfulness for our active, engaged participation in the more-than-human world.

From dualism to a world with heart

Scholars note that before the modern era (that is, before the seventeenth century) this concept of the heart as the expression of the depth and wholeness of being was commonplace in biblical and Christian thought. It was only with the emergence of the

---

3. Robert Sardello, *Heartfulness*, Pocket Edition (Gainesville, TX: Golden-stone Press, 2017), 3.

modern form of dualism, which envisioned a gap between body and soul and between heart and mind, that the heart was identified as just one of the interior faculties.[4] In our own era, sometimes termed "postmodern" to indicate that the assumptions that constituted modernity are fading, there is an effort to reclaim a sense of the wholeness of body-mind-spirit. As noted in the Introduction, stories of heart-wholeness may not be entirely new (e.g., they have predecessors in ancient traditions) but they need major renewal to function well in our postmodern times.

The breakdown of modern dualism is bringing us to a rediscovery of how radically human beings, in all our dimensions of body, mind, and spirit, are immersed in the dynamic web of interconnections that we call "Earth." A thought experiment might help us to see this. Imagine taking a video of a year of your life—all twenty-four hours, every day. Then imagine speeding it up so that each day passes in a minute or so. The rhythm of day and night, activity and rest, would look like a steady heartbeat. We would also see a continuous pulsing movement of food brought from many parts of the Earth entering the body and waste passing out of it into sewers, treatment plants, and on into rivers, lakes, and oceans. Although such a video could only show the gross (in more senses than one!) movements of food and waste, it would graphically reveal how our bodies are completely interdependent with the physical systems of the Earth. Our bodies are, in fact, a recycled form of soil and water. We are the Earth, made capable of thought and speech.

Lest we still think of ourselves as a singular and separated species, it is worth pondering the fact that literally trillions of microorganisms live on and in the human body, outnumber-

---

4. M. Meslin, "Heart," in *Encyclopedia of Religion* (New York: Macmillan, 1987).

ing human cells ten to one.[5] The vast majority of these microorganisms on our skin and in our inner organs are either essential to our health or benign symbiotes. The average human has three to four pounds of bacteria in their gut, and we would not be able to digest our food or synthesize essential nutrients without them. We generally become aware of our tiny companions only in the rare case that one of their species contributes to noticeable illness or imbalance. Medical researchers now suspect that modern medicine's carpet-bombing approach to getting rid of these few pathological microorganisms may actually be damaging to the entire bodily ecosystem, contributing to the modern epidemics of obesity, diabetes, hypertension, depression, and other chronic diseases. In fact, our bodies are a community of interdependent living organisms; and bodily communities, like social communities, flourish when diversity is nourished.

This account of our bodies as microbial communities is only one small aspect of the widening circles of our enmeshment in living communities of mutual sustenance. We are interdependent with all other participants in the stream of life, from its tiniest microbial members to the myriads of plants, fungi, insects, and animals. Ecopsychologist Andy Fisher asserts that maturing as a participant in this life-stream means "graduating into ever-widening spheres of social belonging" with all its other members. Our humanity, concludes Fisher, "is incomplete until we have established our kinship or social relations with the larger natural world and so satisfied our longing to feel at home in or at peace with the cosmos as a whole." The highest maturity is to know one's kinship—one's relational belonging and care—with those who may superficially appear most

---

5. Ed Yong, *I Contain Multitudes: The Microbes within Us and a Grander View of Life* (Ecco—an imprint of HarperCollins Publishers, 2016).

unlike oneself.[6] By this definition, most of us today are not very far along on the scale of human and Earth-community maturity.

If we spend time reflecting on the reality that we are the Earth and that our bodies are a community of organisms, we will discover that our heart is deeply implicated in these webs of relationships. All the Earth goes with us as we enter the interiority of our heart and discover its depths; in such moments the Earth is realizing its own potential of interiority. We are bonded with Earth places and Earth creatures, some consciously (e.g., our home, family, friends, and pets) and many unconsciously (the air, water, sun, soil), and innumerable living creatures who participate in nourishing us). We belong ineluctably to the Earth community, as we may become aware in moments of delight in what we call "nature." And Earth means everything to us—even though we usually take it for granted and forget that this web of relations requires our active participation and care. Our heart, in all its dimensions, relies on and finds its life in the community of Earth. The wager of this book is that this is not a one-way relationship. Our world, too, has a Heart.

The Heart of Jesus

In this book the basis for that wager is being developed in relation to traditions surrounding the Heart of Jesus. Earlier, we described how our human hearts partake of physical, affective, and spiritual dimensions, always situated in a multifaceted ecology of relationships. When we affirm that Jesus is human, we presume that he shared in all these dimensions of heart-experience. When we affirm that he is divine, we see him im-

---

6. Andy Fisher, *Radical Ecopsychology: Psychology in the Service of Life*, 2nd ed., SUNY Series in Radical Social and Political Theory (Albany: State University of New York Press, 2013), 122, 138–39.

buing them in some mysterious way with yet another level of profundity. Jean Eudes, who was one of the major seventeenth-century propagators of the Sacred Heart devotion, wrote about the "three hearts" of Jesus as the physical heart, the spiritual heart, and the divine heart. Some of the theology around his teaching is a bit outdated, so here I will try to articulate what Eudes's concept of the three dimensions of Jesus's heart could look like in dialogue with today's ecological theology.

The physical heart of Jesus is the living, pulsing organ that was constructed with the same molecules of oxygen and carbon and hydrogen and nitrogen that circulated for eons before his birth and still circulate today, in us and in every member of the Earth community. This heart beats at the center of the physicality of his—and our—relation of kinship with all life. This incarnate, physical heart grounds what Pope Francis's 2015 encyclical *Laudato' Si* affirms: "The entire material universe speaks of God's love, his boundless affection for us. Soil, water, mountains: everything is, as it were, a caress of God."[7]

The second dimension of Jesus's heart is the infinitely tender, compassionate, merciful, companioning heart that he offers to every living being. We say, "Were not our hearts burning within us?" (Luke 24:32) when we are aware of this indwelling fire. In those moments we know and delight in the truth of our kinship with him and with all creation. John of the Cross described such a heart-experience thus:

> The soul feels its ardor strengthen and increase [until] seemingly there flow seas of loving fire within it, reaching to the heights and depths of the earthly and heavenly spheres, imbuing all with love. It seems to it that the entire universe is

7. Pope Francis, *On Care for Our Common Home: Laudato Si'* (Washington, DC: United States Conference of Catholic Bishops, 2015), para. 84.

a sea of love in which it is engulfed, for conscious of the living point or center of love within itself, it is unable to catch
sight of the boundaries of this love.[8]

Finally, there is the divine and cosmic heart of Jesus—the
Heart that is one with the Father and the Spirit, the cosmic
Christ whose living heart is the pattern and pulse at the foundation of all creation. In the words of Colossians 1:15: "He is
the image of the invisible God, the firstborn of all creation; for
in him all things in heaven and on earth were created, things
visible and invisible...." Another famous expression of this is
the last line of Dante's *Paradiso*: "Now my desire and will were
turned...by the Love that moves the sun and other stars." The
Heart that touches our heart and sets it on fire is the same
Heart that moves the stars and galaxies and infinite reaches of
space. The centuries-long Catholic tradition of devotion to the
Sacred Heart, which we will review more closely in the next
chapter, is directed to this three-dimensioned "Heart at the
heart of the world."

Why devotion?

The underlying Latin meaning of "devotion" is "consecration."
It refers to an earnest, fervent, faithful dedication to a person,
practice, or cause. Like all words, its usage and nuances differ
in varying eras and cultures. In the Roman Catholic context,
the term "devotions" has come to refer to popular customs and
practices, often elaborately involving the body and the senses,
by which people express ardent faith apart from the institutionalized form of the liturgy. While "popular piety" and "de-

8. John of the Cross, *Living Flame of Love*, trans. Kieran Kavanaugh and
Otilio Rodriguez, rev. ed, Collected Works of Saint John of the Cross (Washington, DC: Institute of Carmelite Studies, 1991), 661.

votions" are not completely synonymous, both derive from the creativity of ordinary people as they strive to inculturate and personalize faith into tangible, accessible forms. The centralized institutional Church is always on the alert to rein in devotions, trying to ensure that they remain linked to the liturgy and that they do not stray from promoting correct doctrinal teaching. Since devotions and popular piety originate from "below," however, it is part of their nature to overflow boundaries and reinterpret doctrines in ways that make sense within the worldview of people at the grassroots.

Devotions are often especially prominent in the lives of people who are oppressed, marginalized, or displaced. When Western missionaries brought Christianity to indigenous cultures around the world, usually doing so in the company of highly oppressive and exploitative empire-builders from the missionaries' European nations, the people often responded by syncretizing their ancient symbols, rituals, and customs with the imported ones. A well-known example of this is the apparition of Our Lady of Guadalupe to Juan Diego at Tepeyac, an indigenous holy place, in the form of a young Indian woman adorned with the symbols of Juan Diego's Chichimec culture. Similarly, Mexican Day of the Dead altars and rituals appear to combine Aztec customs with those of the Europe-based All Saints Day feast. Scholars studying the devotions practiced at Miami's Nuestra Señora de Caridad shrine find that these rituals enable Cuban Americans to maintain and celebrate their attachment to their native land while building a life in exile.[9] The monarchists who resisted the secularization of France in the nineteenth century made the devotion to the Sacred Heart central to their political identity. Wendy Wright observes that in

---

9. Thomas A. Tweed, *Our Lady of the Exile: Diasporic Religion at a Cuban Catholic Shrine in Miami*, Religion in America Series (New York: Oxford University Press, 1997).

addition to ethnic minorities and oppressed peoples, today it is "those conservative groups who feel their world has been co-opted by Vatican II"[10] who most fervently promote devotions as a way of affirming identity while experiencing marginalization.

Thus, devotional practice can function in a variety of ways, including bridging two cultures, recreating a threatened communal identity, resisting co-optation by a perceived oppressor, or pumping up the affective energy felt for a political cause. Let us not forget, however, that at the center of devotion is always the heart. All that has been said about the place and functions of the heart can be applied to our understanding of devotional practices. Devotions express personal, heartfelt love; as such, they enhance the person's lived experience of interiority, bonding, belonging, and meaning. It is not surprising that the symbol of the heart itself has become the focus of so much devotion.

Devotion, of course, does not take place in some rarified, purely "spiritual" form; it occurs in the midst of real people's lives with all their individual idiosyncrasies, psychological traumas, cultural preferences, and investment in political battles. This is why the "same" devotion, such as the devotion to the Sacred Heart, does not remain the same from century to century or from culture to culture. In the next chapter we will take a brief tour through some of the patterns that Christian heart-devotion has taken in different eras and cultures.

Selfhood and personhood

Talk about the "heart" is often more poetic and rhetorical than philosophically precise. In this book I am not attempting a full

---

10. Wendy M. Wright, "'I Blessed the Tattoo': Reflections on Spirituality and Popular Devotions," *Spiritus: A Journal of Christian Spirituality* 17, no. 1 (2017): 91, https://doi.org/10.1353/scs.2017.0005.

philosophical or theological development of the concept, since the intent of the book is to offer an evocative and inspiring vision rather than a rigorous scholarly monograph. Nonetheless, for those interested in going a bit deeper into the issues, it will be helpful to make some more distinctions. I have referred above to "heart-stories," meaning the narratives formed from deep emotions and memories that pattern our lives. At least two distinct dimensions, however, feed into our heart-stories. The stories that run in our minds and hearts are constructions of our self-protective selfhood, and (at least potentially) expressions of our self-giving personhood.[11]

First, "selfhood" is an ever-restless process of construction of identity based on self-awareness and aimed at maintaining one's integrity, coherence, and social esteem. Kenneth Schmitz wrote that the way of selfhood is that of "a resilient insistence upon an identity that preserves itself against others."[12] Thus, the "selfing" process is fundamentally self-centered (though not in a pejorative sense) and self-protective. It is as necessary to competent psychological function as having a skeleton is to walking. To fail to develop an adequately coherent and self-protective self is a severe pathology, and likely to result in behavior destructive to oneself and others.

The consensus today is to see the self as heavily invested in the story-telling process. The purpose of this self-story is to interpret past, present, and imagined future in a way that maintains an inner sense of continuity, integrity, and meaningfulness while contributing to the fulfillment of one's social and material

---

11. Mary Frohlich, "The Vulnerable (Post) Modern Self and the 'Greening' of Spiritual Personhood through Life in the Spirit," *Religions* (Basel, Switzerland) 11, no. 4 (2020): 19–34, https://doi.org/10.3390/rel 11040194.

12. Kenneth L. Schmitz, "Selves and Persons: A Difference in Loves?" *Communio* 18 (1991): 185.

goals. Despite the aim of coherence and continuity, this story-telling process is actually highly responsive to changing relation-ships and circumstances. This means that there is likely to be more than one story line in process, and even within a given story line reinterpretation is constantly going on based on new circumstances or new goals.

"Personhood," however, refers to a relational center that exists to be in communion with other persons. The most central characteristic of personhood is that persons exist only in a free and mutual relationship of love with other persons.[13] This definition of personhood arose within the Christian tradition as a way of understanding divine three- and-oneness. Person-hood, therefore, is not to be understood as a "deeper level" of selfhood, nor is it a distinct identifiable "place" or "function" within natural entities. Rather, it is an apophatic participation of creatures in the personal reality of God. The personal God freely embraces all of creation in loving relationship, and each creature is formed in some degree of capacity to mediate that personhood. Persons love, not for any extrinsic reason, but simply because being a person is to love. We will explore later on in the book what it might mean not to limit personhood to human beings, but to recognize elements of it in other liv-ing creatures or perhaps even more broadly, in all of created reality.

Personhood, then, is fundamentally relational and self-donative. It is not an achievement, but a given dimension of our createdness. A newborn, for example, is already a person. As parents attest, babies love, and call forth love, at the most profound level. It usually requires a lifetime of commitment to spiritual practice, however, to bring forth the full flowering of

---

13. Catherine Mowry LaCugna, *God for Us: The Trinity and Christian Life* (San Francisco, CA: HarperSanFrancisco, 1991), 289–92.

personhood in (relatively) selfless loving. I say "relatively" because it is obvious that real human beings are always operating in both of these dimensions. Every human act deploys a complex dynamic of self-protection (selfhood) and self-giving (personhood).

Heartfulness and hope

Heart-experience, I propose, is where our self-giving personhood and our self-protective selfhood come together in a holistic way in real life circumstances. Thus, to live "heartfully" is to live our self-story from the depth and fullness of our relational personhood rather than from the narcissism of the surface of life. The challenge of our time is that our very survival as a species is calling for a vastly broadened and deepened level of relationality—one that reaches out to interact respectfully and appropriately with all other species, geological processes, and the Earth itself by including them as our "kin." To maintain the Earth community as a richly biodiverse ecosystem at this point in history demands that we be persons—that is, creatures defined by, and living to the full, our capacity for relationality and self-giving love—in a fresh and profound manner.

Yet in this moment of Earth crisis, the predominant style of human self-making instead seems to be tending more strongly toward superficiality, fragmentation, and narcissism. Is it possible for such weak and broken selves to rediscover and develop the relational potential of their personhood? Within the conditions of the dawning Anthropocene, can the double dynamic of self-protection and self-giving be opened up in a way that more effectively protects human and other life on Earth? This would require, it seems, harnessing afresh both the self-protective and the self-giving potentials of human beings.

Currently, human self-making—that is, the motivating stories we tell—is failing to fulfill the function of protecting human life and legacy beyond the present generation. The fatal vulnerability is that of modernity: the separation of the self from its integral connection with the natural world. What seems to be happening at the dawn of the Anthropocene is that both separated partners—Earth and human selves—are spiraling in tandem toward destructive, out-of-control "overheating." For the Earth, the spiral of overheating is the intensification of pollution, climate change, and ecosystem fragmentation. For humans, the spiral of overheating is a style of selfhood that has lost touch with both inner and outer sources of meaning, stability, and resilience. These two spirals are feeding each other, with increasingly deadly consequences.

Yet this emerging Anthropocene era of deep human impact on Earth processes may still be able to give birth to another possibility. Can we humans recalibrate our self-making to express more fully the capacities of our personal responsiveness to the Earth processes with which we are, in fact, completely interdependent? Frederick Buechner famously said that vocation is "where your deep gladness and the world's deep hunger meet."[14] In that perspective, heartfulness is giving our unique gift in a way that both fulfills us and builds love more fully into the world. This is what Joanna Macy calls "the greening of the self,"[15] and it appears to be the only scenario in which our Earth can be sustained as habitat for humans (and vast numbers of other species) for more than a few more decades. My proposal is that the path to hope is making our own the

---

14. Frederick Buechner, *Wishful Thinking: A Seeker's ABC*, rev. and expanded ed. (San Francisco: HarperSanFrancisco, 1993), 119.

15. Joanna Macy, *World as Lover, World as Self: Courage for Global Justice and Ecological Renewal* (Berkeley: Parallax Press, 2007).

4

story of living heartfully as kin and community members within the human and more-than-human worlds. That vision is what this book aims to develop.

FOR REFLECTION AND PRACTICE:

Reflect on all your relationships and interdependences. Expand your reflection beyond the human to include places, ecosystems, air and water, animals, plants, microbes, and whatever else come to mind. How do these relationships enrich your life? How do they make you vulnerable?

What does "heart" mean for you? Close your eyes and feel that meaning in your body. Where is "heart" located for you? What is its relation to the beating of your physical heart?

FOR FURTHER READING:

Gail Godwin, *Heart: A Personal Journey through Its Myths and Meanings* (New York: HarperCollins, 2001).
David Richo, *The Sacred Heart of the World: Restoring Mystical Devotion to Our Spiritual Life* (Mahwah, NJ: Paulist, 2007).
Robert Sardello, *Heartfulness* (School of Spiritual Psychology, 2017).

2

Constellations of Heart Devotion

Devotion to the Heart of Jesus has been perennial within Christian tradition. It is one of the core ways in which Christians have sought heartful stories that meet the self-protective needs of their era while engaging their self-giving personhood to the full. In a fascinating 2021 book, anthropologist Marion Dapsance provides an in-depth study of the modern history and recent reinvention of this devotion in France. In her conclusion, she uses the image of "constellations" to describe the many variations of the devotion to Christ's Heart.[1] Christian revelation, she proposes, can be compared to the stars in the sky. The stars are the manifestations of the fundamental truths of revelation. Some stars are easily visible, while the presence of others has taken much time and labor to be brought to the fore. From ancient times people have looked at the stars, observed patterns, and told stories about these heavenly constellations. The patterns and stories change, however, depending both on which stars are seen and on the interpreter's personal and cultural repertoire.

---

1. Marion Dapsance, *Le Sacré-Coeur et La Réinvention Du Christianisme* (Montrouge: Bayard, 2021), 339–49.

The devotion to the Sacred Heart, Dapsance suggests, is not a "star" (a fundamental truth of revelation) but rather a grouping of stars into a constellation (an interpretive story that offers practical spiritual benefit). However, the groupings and the interpretations have changed considerably over time, depending on the available symbolic structures and needs of each historical era. In this chapter we review some of these constellations, with an eye to both what they offer to us today and why we are in need of a new constellation in order to respond adequately to the current crisis of the Earth. In this brief survey, it will not be possible to cover all the variations. What we can learn, however, is how this archetypal form of devotion has repeatedly been re-visioned in new forms to meet new needs. This will aid us as we consider whether it may yet rise again in our own time.

The first five centuries

An utterly central issue during the first five centuries after Jesus's death was how to understand and articulate who he was. The earliest Christians knew he was human, but were convinced he was divine as well. As time went on the balance shifted, and doubts were raised about whether he was really human. The writings of the New Testament and of those we term "Fathers of the Church" strive for effective ways to portray Jesus as both human and divine. It is in this context that we can best understand the earliest Christian reflections on the Heart of Christ.

In the Bible, *kardia* or "heart" refers not to the physical organ but to the center of a person's life, with special focus on intellect, emotions, and will. The New Testament does not use the word *kardia* with reference to Jesus. Within a few centuries, however, certain texts had been identified as evoking rich meditations on his heart, both in its physical manifestation and as the spiritual center of his being. First there is John

19:34–35, the story of the centurion piercing Jesus's side on the cross so that blood and water flow out. The implication, although not stated in so many words, is that the lance pierces Jesus's physical heart, which is the source of the fount of blood and water. This text harks back to Zechariah 12:10, "They will look on the one whom they have pierced." Nearby in Zechariah 13:1 we also note the line: "On that day a fountain will be opened for the house of David and for the inhabitants of Jerusalem, to purify from sin and uncleanness." Another text that was brought into the same orbit was John 7:38, "Rivers of living water shall flow from within him." The Greek word that is used in this text for "within" is *koilias*. Its literal meaning is "abdomen" or "belly," but a good figurative translation would be "heart." As witnessed also by 1 John 5:6–8, the Ephesian tradition of John the Evangelist equates the blood and water with the Spirit that is poured out on the Church through the pierced Heart of Jesus on the cross.[2]

It did not take long for others to expand upon these images using the allegorical methods of their time. Irenaeus (130–202) called the Church "the fountain of the living water that flows to us from the Heart of Christ," and opined that a person "who has no part in this Spirit will receive no nourishment or life at the breast of our mother Church."[3] Origen (185–253) meditated on John 7:38 as referring to the Heart of Christ, his "innermost self, the source of thoughts and of wisdom, from which the true gnostic, the mystically favored [person] of the spirit, drinks the living water of wisdom."[4] He and others also

---

2. Josef Stierli, ed., *Heart of the Saviour: A Symposium on Devotion to the Sacred Heart* (New York: Herder and Herder, 1958), 34.

3. Stierli, *Heart of the Saviour*, 44.

4. Stierli, *Heart of the Saviour*, 41.

drew in other biblical texts, such as the rock that Moses struck to bring forth water in the desert (Exodus 17:6; Numbers 20:11) and the holy city where God dwells and a river of life-giving water flows forth to rejuvenate the Earth (Revelation 22:1). Tertullian (155–220) initiated a tradition of seeing the water as symbolizing the sacrament of baptism, and the blood the sacrament of the Eucharist.

In the fourth and fifth centuries, other authors wove connections to yet more scripture passages. Ambrose (340–397) wrote of Jesus as the grape-laden vine (John 15), pierced so that the living water would flow forth on our behalf. Augustine (354–430) also added a meditation on the story of John leaning on Jesus's breast at the last supper (John 13:25), asserting that it was because John drank from the breast of Jesus that he could give us to drink though his gospel. Peter Chrysologus (406–450) reflected on Thomas putting his hand into Jesus's side, touching the wounds that pour forth faith upon the whole world (John 20:24–29).[5] Drawing on Paul's theology of Christ as the second Adam (1 Corinthians 15:45–49), another set of writers contemplated the Church being born from the opening in Christ's side as Eve had been born from the opened side of Adam. The Heart was then interpreted as a maternal womb, bearing and giving birth to the Church through Christ's wounded side.

Through the focus on the heart, all these early reflections succeed in emphasizing Jesus's physical humanity, bleeding and dying on the cross, while at the same time effectively portraying him as the divine source of the Church, faith, sacraments, and all the fruits of the outpoured Spirit.

---

5. Margaret A. Williams, *The Sacred Heart in the Life of the Church* (New York: Sheed and Ward, 1957), chap. 3.

Medieval mystics

In the medieval period in Europe, the Church and its core doctrines were so well established that they permeated daily life as
well as social, cultural, and governmental structures. Although
theological debates certainly continued, the really existential
issue for those with a particularly fervent desire to follow
Christ wholeheartedly was how to access Christ beyond the all-
encompassing customs and routines provided by the Church.
The great mystical traditions of the Sacred Heart developed in
this context, mainly among those living in monasteries. Here
we have space to review only a few of the major figures.

Bernard of Clairvaux (1090–1153), who founded the Bene-
dictine reform known as the Cistercians, is noted for boldly
claiming the affective intensity of his love for the human
Christ. Reading the love story of the Song of Songs, he wrote
movingly of Christ's tender love and exclaimed: "The secret of
his Heart lies visible through the cleft of his Body; visible too
the great mystery of his love, and the bowels of his mercy."[6] His
friend and disciple William of St. Thierry (1085–1148) added:
"We enter totally into your Heart, O Jesus.... Open, Lord, the
lateral door of your ark, so that your elect can enter.... Open
the side of your body, so that those may enter who desire to see
the secrets of the Son." [This is an allusion to Noah opening the
side of the ark so the animals to be saved could enter.][7] The
wide influence of Bernard and William led to many other
monastic authors taking up the theme as well.

---

6. *Sermo in Cantico LXI, 4 (P.L. 183, 1072).*

7. Pierre Debongnie, "Commencement et Recommencements de la
Dévotion au Coeur de Jésus," *Études Carmélitaines* 29, Le Coeur (1950): 172.

Following the conventions of the genres in which they were trained, the patristic and medieval male clerics whose works we have been reviewing up to this point do not speak directly of their personal experience of the Heart, whether they had such an experience or not. Instead, they express their devotion by eloquently weaving together meditations on scripture texts. It is with the female Cistercian Lutgarde of Aywières (1182–1246) that devotion to the Heart departs from these confines to become a living exchange.

Lutgarde was about to become the fiancée of a young man when Christ appeared to her, opened his chest, and told her to seek only pure love. After she entered the monastery, he invited her to exchange hearts with him, thus initiating a tradition in which a number of subsequent devotees of the Heart would participate. It may have been a reflection on Ezekiel 36:26, where God promises "a new heart and a new spirit," that inspired this experience, in which Jesus removed Lutgarde's human heart and replaced it with his own. On another occasion, Christ appeared to her covered with blood on the cross. He detached one arm from the cross, embraced her against his right side, and applied her mouth to his wound so that she could drink from it. Although drinking from the Heart of Christ had been alluded to by earlier writers, it is only with Lutgarde that it begins to be portrayed as an embodied experience of the utmost intimacy.

Like Lutgarde, Gertrude of Helfta (1256–1302) found herself invited to exchange her heart with that of Jesus. On one occasion she saw the Lord extending his Heart to her, then drawing it in with her inside it so that she entered fully into him. Later, she asserted that the five wounds of Christ were mystically inscribed on her own heart. Another time, a golden tube extended from his Heart to hers, making a channel through which the Lord could pour forth his grace to others.

She felt the sweetness and grace of the Holy Spirit coming forth from the Heart of Jesus like a stream of honey, filling her heart with a torrent of delight. She also received the transpiercing of her heart by a "ray of light flowing from the divine wound … drawing to himself all my desires in an unspeakable sweetness."[8]

Many other female mystics of this period shared in similar experiences. Catherine of Siena (1347–1380) is another who experienced the exchange of hearts. Meditating on John 20:27–28, the story of Thomas being invited to put his hand into the wound in Jesus's side, she recounted graphic experiences of being drawn into the wound in Jesus's side and blissfully embraced within his heart. She taught that we nurse at the breast of charity, which is the Heart of Christ crucified, but that "we cannot drink from the heart of Christ unless we are willing also to drink from the wounds of our neighbors! And when we do, we ourselves become sources of that same nourishment for others."[9] When she asked Jesus why his heart had to be pierced, he answered: "My longing for humankind was infinite, but the actual deed of bearing pain and torment was finite and could never show all the love I had. This was why I wanted you to see my inmost heart, so that you would see that I loved you more than finite sufferings could show."[10]

In the experiences of these female mystics, images such as those of the thrusting lance and the vulva-like opening from which a child is born, and into which one is drawn to enter with utmost delight, often gained a quite explicit erotic undertone. A

---

8. Debongnie, "Commencement et Recommencements de la Dévotion au Coeur de Jésus," 170.

9. Suzanne Noffke, *Catherine of Siena: Vision through a Distant Eye* (New York: Authors Choice Press, 2006), 29.

10. Catherine of Siena, *The Dialogue*, ed. Suzanne Noffke, The Classics of Western Spirituality (Mahwah, NJ: Paulist Press, 1980), 138–39.

tradition of "nuptial mysticism" emerged, envisioning Jesus
and his devotee engaged in a spousal relationship that culmi-
nates in spiritual marriage and ecstatic experiences of union.
While nuptial imagery places a strong premium on these stories
of fulfillment and delight, it typically also places an equally
strong premium on graphic participation in the sufferings of
Christ. Thus, devotion to the Heart of Christ and devotion to
his wounds have long been profoundly intertwined, and more
often than not invested with an intense erotic charge as well.

It is important to note here that asserting an erotic dimension in spiritual experience is not the same as reducing spirituality to sublimated sexual desire. To quote Simone Weil:

> To reproach mystics with loving God by means of the fac-
> ulty of sexual love is as though one were to reproach a
> painter with making pictures by means of colors composed
> of material substances. We haven't anything else with which
> to love.[11]

The erotic, as we will see later on, is not limited to its obvious role in romantic and sexual love. It is the longing of the
whole, heartful person to participate fully in mutually loving
relationships. During the medieval period, Heart devotion developed this to a peak of intensity.

Seventeenth-century France

It was in seventeenth-century France, just at the dawn of
the modern era, that the next great blossoming of devotion
to Christ's Heart took place. This was a century in which
there was an intense fascination with all aspects of the

---

11. Simone Weil, *The Notebooks of Simone Weil*, trans. Arthur Wills
(London: Routledge and Kegan Paul, 1956), 2:472.

heart, including both its physiology and its role in human affective and spiritual life.[12] It even became popular to cut out and preserve the physical hearts of persons who were regarded as powerful or holy, so that they could be displayed as a particularly potent form of relic. It may have been partly as a reaction to the rise of the "heartless" tendencies of the new scientific and philosophical ideas emerging in that period that spiritual guides and teachers felt such an intense need to renovate Heart devotion.

In a period when the rise of humanism was calling for greater attention to the affirmation of human capabilities and, at the same time, the demand for religious reform was at its peak, Francis de Sales (1567–1622) developed a fresh way to place the "exchange of hearts" between human persons and God at the center of Christian spirituality. This mystical motif, says Wendy Wright, "was by de Sales effectively interiorized, secularized, laicized, and embedded in a biblically based, theologically rich mysticism of apostolic service."[13] Thus, Francis de Sales was able to renovate Heart devotion to respond to the mentality of the emerging modern period.

The Salesians' scriptural watchword is Jesus's invitation, "Come to me and learn from me, for I am gentle and humble of heart' (Matthew 11:28–30), while their motto is "Live Jesus!" The devotee becomes aligned to the rhythm of God's Heart by practicing the two arms of love—love of God and love of neigh-

---

12. Ted Campbell, *The Religion of the Heart: A Study of European Religious Life in the Seventeenth and Eighteenth Centuries* (Eugene: Wipf and Stock Publishers, 2000).

13. Wendy M. Wright, "He Opened His Side: Francis de Sales and the Exchange of Divine and Human Hearts," in *Mysticism and Contemporary Life: Essays in Honor of Bernard McGinn*, ed. John J. Markey and J. August Higgins (New York: Crossroad, 2019), 109.

bor. Salesian spirituality is optimistic, affirming that God has created the universe to manifest love and that Jesus's Heart is the fullest manifestation of this. Since our human hearts are built for love, following the natural orientation of our hearts will lead us to goodness and, ultimately, through grace, to the Heart of God. All hearts find their unity, their joy, and their fulfillment in the tender Heart of Christ, who is the one heart and soul of all creation. Along with Jeanne de Chantal (1572–1641), Francis de Sales promoted the practice of the "little virtues" of gentleness, kindness, humility, simplicity, and friendship. These practices are available to anyone, laity as well as clergy, women as well as men, and poor laborers as well as nobles. Through them, the gentle Heart of Jesus gradually becomes one's own heart. In this way one truly learns to "Live Jesus."

A bit later in the century, Jean Eudes (1601–1680) made the Hearts of Jesus and Mary the center of his preaching and his theology. As a young man Eudes joined the Oratory, a community of priests that had been instituted by Pierre de Bérulle (1575–1629). Bérulle, disturbed by the anthropocentrism of emerging modernity, called for a "Copernican revolution" that would radically recenter the Christian spiritual life around the grandeur and sanctity of the Incarnate Word. He taught that our own holiness depends on uniting ourselves to the interior dispositions and attitudes (or "states," in his vocabulary) of Jesus, the perfect adorer of God. Just as the Word radically emptied himself in becoming human, so too we must be emptied and annihilated in our own preferences and will. When the union is complete, we will truly be able to say that "It is no longer I who live, but Christ who lives in me" (Galatians 2:20).

Jean Eudes embraced this spirituality but gave it a more joyful, personalistic tone by centering all his thought around the concept of "the heart." He was strongly influenced by Marie des Vallées, a middle-aged peasant woman whose convulsions and visions led many to regard her as in need of exorcism. She shared her visions with Eudes, who came to believe in her. In one vision, Jesus told Marie that he had three hearts, Charity, his Passion, and the Blessed Sacrament, and that they are all one Heart. In another, Jesus told her that he had inspired the feast of the Heart of Mary and that those opposed to it would be punished. In his subsequent ministry and writings Eudes integrated these ideas with his Bérullian theology, producing several theologically well-grounded texts on the Hearts of Jesus and Mary.

Taking up the idea of the "three hearts," Eudes articulated it in three forms: the three hearts of the Trinity, the three hearts of Christ, and the three hearts of Mary. In regard to the Trinity, he wrote:

> The first heart of the Trinity is the Son of God, who is the heart of the Father ... The second is the Holy Spirit, who is the heart of the Father and Son. The third is divine love, which is the heart of the Father, the Son, and the Holy Spirit.[14]

Jesus's three hearts are the heart at the center of his physical body; the feeling heart that constitutes the center of his soul; and the divine Heart, which is the Holy Spirit. Mary is the perfect adorer of Jesus, which means that her own will is annihilated and her heart is completely at one with that of the Incarnate Word. Mary, then, also has three hearts, all centered in those of Jesus: her physical heart, her spiritual heart, and the Heart of Jesus.

Jean Eudes's other major contribution is as author of liturgical texts celebrating the Hearts of Jesus and Mary. After twenty years as an Oratorian, he left to found his own Congre-

---

14. William M. Thompson, *Bérulle and the French School: Selected Writings*, The Classics of Western Spirituality (Mahwah, NJ: Paulist, 1989), 328.

gation of Jesus and Mary (commonly called the Eudists). In that community he composed numerous offices and mass texts, many of which received approbation for local usage. These were adopted by various dioceses and national churches throughout the world, thus laying the groundwork for the eventual institution of the universal feast (later solemnity) of the Sacred Heart of Jesus in 1856 and of the Immaculate Heart of Mary in 1944.

Marguerite Marie Alacoque

Francis de Sales and Jean Eudes offer compelling spiritual stories of the Heart of Christ. Yet these stories are far less well-known than the story of the Sacred Heart that was promoted by the French Visitation nun Marguerite Marie Alacoque (1647–1690). She had a troubled childhood that included very difficult relationships with relatives, serious problems with eating, a tendency to go overboard with corporal mortification, and several health crises. As a nun, she was exposed to the teachings of Francis de Sales as well as to the traditions of nuptial mysticism, especially that of Gertrude of Helfta.

Between 1573 and 1575, Marguerite Marie experienced a number of visions in which Jesus showed her his Heart as a blazing furnace of love for human beings. He told her that his Heart is deeply wounded, however, by human indifference, and especially that of those who have been chosen and consecrated to adore God. He announced to Marguerite that the Sacred Heart had especially chosen her to reveal the secret of his love and to transmit it to the entire world. Those who welcome this message will console him and repair the offenses of others. Very specifically, the visions asked for the practices of the Holy Hour on Thursday evening, communion on First Fridays, and the institution of the Feast of the Sacred Heart in the universal Church.

Marguerite's community and spiritual advisors initially did not find her visions convincing. The arrival of Claude de la Colombière (1641–1682) as superior of the Jesuit community in Paray, however, changed her fate. The two felt an immediate rapport, and he quickly joined her in believing in and promoting the content of her visions. From then on this form of devotion to the Sacred Heart was closely allied with the Jesuits, who helped to spread it around the world. They also were instrumental in linking it to the theology of reparation. The concept of reparation was drawn from the juridical language of the time, which asserted that if a person subject to the king (or another high-ranking person) failed to give him the honor he was due, that person was required to make reparation. Theologically, reparation became a ritualized juridical act that, because it is costly and humiliating for the sinner, restores God's honor.[15]

Especially between about 1750 and 1950, Marguerite Marie's form of devotion to the Sacred Heart enjoyed massive popularity in many parts of the Catholic world. Since the Second Vatican Council (1962–1965), however, that popularity has undergone a startling decline. While no doubt a significant number of people still find Marguerite Marie's piety and recommended practices deeply meaningful, it seems clear that this form of heart spirituality is not in sync with many aspects of contemporary mentality.

One reason for this is that Marguerite seemed to revel in suffering and humiliation, even going so far as to taste vomit and feces in order to abase herself. Moreover, the concept of "reparation" that became closely associated with her form of the devotion is based on the idea that God is so offended by the

15. Jacques Le Brun, "Une Lecture Historique Des Écrits Des Marguerite-Marie Alacoque," *Nouvelles de l'Institut Catholique de Paris* 1 (1977): 38–53.

failure of people to adequately perform juridical rituals such as attending Sunday worship, giving due honor to the Blessed Sacrament, or slavishly obeying superiors that God requires Jesus and other true lovers of God to suffer horribly to make up for these insults. Today, most people are offended by a concept of a God who desires, enjoys, or demands suffering. Moreover, the top-down, rigid structure of Church, authority, and law presumed by Marguerite does not correspond to the relational expectations of contemporary society.

The development of new "constellations" of the Sacred Heart in France did not stop with Marguerite Marie, although for several centuries most of the new interpretations relied heavily on hers. In the early eighteenth century Bishop Belsunce of Marseilles, facing a devastating pestilence, preached penitential reparation for sin and invocation of the Sacred Heart as the way to be saved from physical disaster. After the French Revolution, defenders of the deposed monarchy amplified the association Marguerite Marie had made between the Sacred Heart and the victory of the French king, Louis XIV, into a full-fledged monarchist and anti-revolutionary ideology. In the middle of the nineteenth century, Léon Dehon (1843–1925) told a story of the reign of the Sacred Heart as the establishment of justice for the poor.

Teilhard de Chardin

The vision of the Sacred Heart found in the writings of the French Jesuit priest Pierre Teilhard de Chardin (1881–1955) comes closest to the one I am developing in this book. From childhood, Teilhard shared his mother's deep devotion to the Sacred Heart of Jesus. At the same time, he also felt deeply drawn to material objects such as stones and bits of iron, in which he sensed a mysterious spiritual presence. During his early years as a Jesuit, he felt increasingly conflicted over the strong natural/supernatural divide that was emphasized in the theology he was being taught. He went on to study for a doctorate in geology and paleontology, thus combining his priesthood with professional work as a scientist.

During his service as a stretcher-bearer during some of the bloodiest battles of World War I, Teilhard experienced intense spiritual growth. In his spiritual autobiography, *The Heart of Matter*, he tells a story about a man going to pray in a small church and seeing a picture of Christ offering his Heart to humanity. The man then has a visionary experience in which an energy emanating from the Heart of Christ vibrates through the whole universe and penetrates to the very core of the viewer's being, "with a full note of explosive bliss that was completely and utterly unique." The man concludes that God is "the Heart of All."[16] Teilhard's secretary and friend, Jeanne Mortier, affirmed that the man was Teilhard himself.[17] Years later, in *The Divine Milieu*, Teilhard wrote of his experience of "the diaphany of the divine at the heart of the universe on fire.... Christ, his heart a fire, capable of penetrating everywhere, and gradually, spreading everywhere."[18]

Increasingly, Teilhard identified the Heart of Christ with what he called the "Omega Point"—the attractive force of infinite divine love that is constantly at work in the created world to lure it toward its "pleroma" or fullness of life. Expressing his personal spirituality, Teilhard wrote:

---

16. Pierre Teilhard de Chardin, *The Heart of Matter* (San Diego: Harcourt Brace Jovanovich, 1978), 65–66.

17. Robert L. Faricy, "The Heart of Christ in the Spirituality of Teilhard de Chardin," *Gregorianum* 69, no. 2 (1988): 275.

18. Pierre Teilhard de Chardin, *The Divine Milieu*, Perennial Classics (New York: Perennial, 2001), 9.

Every exhalation that passes through me, envelops me, or captivates me, emanates, without any doubt, from the heart of God; like a subtle and essential energy, it transmits the pulsations of God's will.... God is at work within life. God helps it, raises it up, gives it the impulse that drives it along, the appetite that attracts it, the growth that transforms it. I can feel God, touch God, "live" God in the deep biological current that runs through my soul and carries it with it.[19]

Thus, Teilhard offers an insightful and inspiring vision of the Heart of Jesus as the heart of matter and of the physical cosmos as Christic. Recently ethicist John P. Slattery has revived a debate about a few ambiguous passages in which Teilhard appears to affirm the inequality of the races and the need for eugenics to enhance the quality of the developing human species.[20] In his response, John F. Haught argues that while these ideas may appear abhorrent today, Teilhard was far from the only theologian of his time who was actively considering them. Even more importantly, the larger vision of Teilhard's thought clearly affirms inclusive divine and human love for the weak and marginalized. The few texts quoted by Slattery do not represent central thrusts for Teilhard, but rather the exploratory forays of a questing mind.[21] Teilhard himself would invite us to focus on developing and enhancing his vision,

---

19. Pierre Teilhard de Chardin, *Writings in Time of War* (New York: Harper & Row, 1968), 60–61.

20. John P. Slattery, "Dangerous Tendencies of Cosmic Theology: The Untold Legacy of Teilhard de Chardin," *Philosophy and Theology* 29, no. 1 (2017): 69–82, https://doi.org/10.5840/philtheol201611971; John P. Slattery, "Pierre Teilhard de Chardin's Legacy of Eugenics and Racism Can't Be Ignored," *Religion Dispatches*, May 2018.

21. John F. Haught, "Trashing Teilhard: How Not to Read a Great Religious Thinker," *Commonweal*, February 19, 2019, https://www.commonweal magazine.org/trashing-teilhard.

rather than canonizing every sentence as if nothing he wrote could ever be critiqued.

.

Other renewal efforts in the twentieth century

Pope Pius XI's 1928 encyclical *Miserentissimus Redemptor* sought to reaffirm the devotion taught by Marguerite Marie Alacoque, especially its emphasis on acts of reparation for injury done to God by sin. In 1956 Pope Pius XII devoted another encyclical, *Haurietis Aquas*, to praise the devotion to the Sacred Heart. Drawing almost entirely upon scriptural, papal, and conciliar texts, along with Thomist theology, he strove to clarify its theological foundations and to reject such criticisms as that it is too sentimental or based too much on the physical dimension. Denying that the source of the devotion was in a woman's visions (i.e., Alacoque), he focused most of his effort on discovering the grounds for Heart devotion in scripture, patristics, and the medieval period. This fervent encyclical has a certain poetic beauty, but the best it can offer in terms of addressing the contemporary world is to inveigh against "godless materialism." By the time the encyclical appeared, popular esteem for devotion to the Sacred Heart was already on the verge of going into free fall.

The great German Jesuit theologian Karl Rahner evinced a lifelong interest in the theology and spirituality of the Sacred Heart. His reflections went through several stages, beginning with retrieving the patristic roots of the devotion and culminating with efforts to think systematically about its relevance for the present and future Church. He developed a theology of the heart as the originating unity from which a person goes forth into the multiplicity of embodied presence and action in the world. The heart is "the point where we border on the mystery of God, the point where we who are from God surrender ourselves to the mystery of God in our original unity or else re-fuse to do so."[22] The Heart of Jesus, Rahner asserted, is "his pri-mal, innermost, formative center (center of the whole man, body and soul, and of his Person, human and divine)."[23] In the open center that is his Heart, Jesus freely surrenders himself to his Father and pours himself out for us and for our redemp-tion. Rahner wrote:

> The only reason we are saved is because the Heart of the In-carnate Word was pierced through and streams of living water flowed from it. The pierced Heart of Jesus Christ is the center of the world in which all the powers and currents of world history are, as it were, bound into one.[24]

In Rahner's view, the context to which Alacoque's "private revelation" was addressed was the emerging secularization of human societies, which is still ongoing. After Vatican II, how-ever, he realized that the devotion to the Sacred Heart as it has been practiced in recent generations (e.g., the form deriving from Alacoque) was fast becoming irrelevant to many. He sug-gested that rather than continuing as a devotion of the masses, it would develop into a special grace given to a few. These few would receive it at the level of their own hearts, in the solitude of the core of their beings, rather than primarily as a commu-nally supported custom. Speaking specifically of the ordained,

---

22. Annice Callahan, *Karl Rahner's Spirituality of the Pierced Heart: A Reinterpretation of Devotion to the Sacred Heart* (Lanham, MD: University Press of America, 1985), 35.

23. Karl Rahner, "Some Theses on the Theology of the Devotion," in *Heart of the Saviour: A Symposium on Devotion to the Sacred Heart,* ed. Josef Stierli (New York: Herder and Herder, 1958), 137.

24. Karl Rahner, *Spiritual Exercises* (New York: Herder and Herder, 1966), 242.

he proposed that the priest of the future should be "a man with the pierced heart because he is to lead men to the very core of their existence, to their inmost heart, because he can only do so if he has found his own heart …"[25] Rahner's vision of the future devotion to the Sacred Heart, then, is that it would be a special gift offered to those who are dedicated to sharing fully in Jesus's life and mission.

Finally, on the level of popular devotion, a new form of Heart devotion emerged with the revelations to the young Polish nun Faustina Kowalska (1905–1938). Even before she entered the convent of the Sisters of Our Lady of Mercy, young Faustina was receiving direct messages from Jesus. Beginning in 1931, she had visions of Christ with rays of red and pale blue light emanating from the location of his heart. Jesus told her to paint the image, that anyone who venerated the image would not perish, and that a feast of Divine Mercy should be instituted on the first Sunday after Easter. Faustina died in 1938 at the age of thirty-three. The Polish Pope John Paul II (papacy 1978–2005) strongly promoted the image and message of Faustina's visions, which he saw as affirmation of the radical character of God's compassion and forgiveness, summed up in the words "Divine Mercy." In 2000, he canonized Faustina and officially instituted the feast of Divine Mercy. While the devotion has gained some popularity, especially among fans of John Paul II, its style and substance remain in the mold of old-style Catholicism rather than breaking new ground.

Conclusion

While these are some of the most prominent stories that have been told about the Heart of Christ, a full accounting would

---

25. Callahan, *Karl Rahner's Spirituality of the Pierced Heart*, 107.

find many others as well.[26] In some sense, they are all "good stories," because each in its own time and place has functioned effectively to provide consolation, guidance, and identity to people who longed to love and serve God. Some of these stories still have much to offer today. Yet the wager of this book is that we are also in need of a new story that looks through the lens of twenty-first century needs at the stars of Christian revelation, and sees them in a new constellation.

FOR REFLECTION AND PRACTICE:

What, if any, is your experience of "devotion to the Sacred Heart"? Journal about your experiences and reactions, both positive and negative.

As you read about these various constellations of Heart devotion, what touched your own heart? Are you drawn to learn more about any of them?

FOR FURTHER READING:

Stephen J. Binz, *The Sacred Heart of Jesus: A Threshold Bible Study* (Mystic, CT: Twenty-Third), 2006.

Margaret A. Williams, *The Sacred Heart in the Life of the Church* (New York: Sheed and Ward, 1957).

Wendy M. Wright, *Sacred Heart: Gateway to God* (Maryknoll, NY: Orbis, 2001).

---

26. Williams, *The Sacred Heart in the Life of the Church*; Wendy M. Wright, *Sacred Heart: Gateway to God* (Maryknoll, NY: Orbis, 2001).

PART TWO

AT THE HEART OF THE WORLD

3

Rediscovering Mother Earth

Not long ago I moved from Chicago, where I had lived for twenty-eight years, to the Boston area. During those many years in Chicago I had devoted long hours and days to getting to know the local flora and fauna, ecological history, and hiking trails. For fifteen of those years I had lovingly cultivated a backyard garden, striving to make it a refuge for native species of insects and birds. I had chosen to move away, knowing that it was time for me to make a fresh start in a new place. Yet I missed the familiarity of the ecosystem that I had left behind. New England was nice enough, but it didn't feel like home.

One pleasantly cold day I went for a walk in a park overlooking the salt marshes of the Weymouth Back River near my residence. As I strolled along, taking notice of the pungent air, the many-colored grasses, and the glint of the sun on the river, I suddenly stopped in my tracks. Deep inside I realized that the Earth itself is "home." The air I breathe, the water that runs in every vein, the dirt from which my bones and flesh are built and rebuilt each and every day—none of these are separate from this air, water, dirt that I see all around me. The Earth embraces me in every dimension, from the surface of my skin to my most intimate interior parts. I am, literally, nothing without Earth! Any "home" that I may find or make is just a little fold in the larger whole. As long as I am on Earth, I am at home.

From the Earth-separated life to naturecentrism

Like most moments of deep insight, the intensity of this experience was fleeting. I returned to my house, where practically everything is designed to shield me from direct participation in the cycles of soil, air, water, and more-than-human living creatures. Walls, windows, and heating and cooling systems make weather only a minimal influence on activity. Most of us react with horror and violence when any insects, mice, bats, or other uninvited creatures encroach upon our assiduously protected dwelling places. Our food arrives in containers and bags, completely disconnected from any soil or living being that actually produced it. Many of these ever-proliferating containers are made of materials deadly to the future of life on Earth. Meanwhile, our bodily waste is flushed away to oblivion, and other waste is encased in plastic bags and piled helter-skelter in the dumpster, soon to disappear into a truck that will take it to the landfill. This "normal" lifestyle both expresses and generates the presumption that modern human life somehow hovers over and apart from the Earth and its cycles, dipping down to use them as desired but not really needing to belong to them.

Criticism of this lifestyle has to be tempered by acknowledgment of its benefits. Those of us fortunate enough to have access to all this protection and labor-saving ease can live longer, healthier, more comfortable lives than were available even to the fabulously wealthy in premodern times. Billions of less fortunate people across the planet ardently aspire to the

pleasures of this way of life. Although even in advanced technological economies a few hardy souls choose to return to the
grueling labor of living off the land, it is unlikely to be the
choice of the masses. It has been noted that in many rural areas
of the United States the long tradition of keeping a vegetable
garden has waned; it is so much easier to buy cheap processed
food than to put in the long hours needed to till, plant, tend,
harvest, and preserve garden produce.

Those of us born to the comforts of the Earth-separated life,
however, have increasingly become aware of its looming
shadow side. Physical health and longevity increase, but at the
cost of a massively expensive medical-industrial complex that
constantly props us up with pharmaceutical and technological
interventions. Research at the Georgetown Health Policy Institute finds that at any given time two-thirds of U.S. adults are
taking at least one prescription drug[1]—artificial chemicals that
pass through us to pollute streams, lakes, and oceans so that
every living creature is being exposed to many of these drugs
willy-nilly. Mental health, meanwhile, is in serious decline, especially among the young. Reasons for this are complex, but
there is strong evidence that an important component of mental health is the felt experience of being close to the Earth and
its creatures. Richard Louv has written of "nature deficit disorder" as a profound dysfunction of modern childhood, in which
many children rarely or never have access to free play in the out-
doors or in even moderately "wild" environments.[2] Spending
time out of doors among green plants and natural sounds has
also proven to have therapeutic benefits for stressed-out adults.

---

1. Health Policy Institute, "Prescription Drugs," https://hpi.georgetown.
edu/rxdrugs/#.

2. Richard Louv, *Last Child in the Woods: Saving Our Children from
Nature-Deficit Disorder*, rev. ed. (Chapel Hill, NC: Algonquin, 2008).

While this approach through examination of the effects of lack of Earth-connection for human health obviously remains very anthropocentric, it is a starting point for a discovery process that often leads people to change some of their most basic assumptions—including anthropocentrism itself. A significant movement of what might be called "naturecentrism" is afoot in the most technology-permeated societies today. It is an effort to reclaim the kind of participatory, mutually respectful, fully embodied, and alive relationship with the Earth and its creatures that we presume (perhaps with a touch of romanticized nostalgia) to have been enjoyed by premodern peoples.

In reality, most adherents to this movement do not actually aspire to going backward to literal imitation of an ancient way of life. Years ago, the philosopher Paul Ricoeur wrote of the developmental process from a naïve mentality that is immersed uncritically in its world to a critical mentality that distances the self and obsessively uses the rational faculty to dissect everything, to a "second naïveté" that reclaims its vital participation in its world while also retaining the ability to question and to maintain appropriate boundaries. Today's naturecentrism seeks a post-critical second naïveté in the relationship of human beings with the natural world.

Mother Earth?

This brings us back to the need for updated stories. As the tragedies of human-induced climate change and massive habitat destruction become ever more evident, many are becoming convinced of the poverty of the colonialist and capitalist assumptions that continue to shape most societal choices. Stories that feature human exceptionalism, hierarchy, and never-ending "progress" are increasingly being rejected. These stories still exercise power, but key elements are being challenged by new scientific insights largely unavailable to earlier generations. For the first time, people are truly aware of the Earth as a small globe in an unimaginably large universe. Awareness is also growing that even though humans manifest a vast diversity of cultures, languages, ethnicities, and histories, all of us are one species on our one and only globe. Rather than being the crown of creation and destined to dominate it, humans are embedded participants in an intricate network of mutual relationships. This awareness of our interdependence with the Earth and its creatures makes the call to renovate old stories for a new consciousness increasingly urgent.

In this context, the old story of "Mother Earth" who gives birth to and nurtures all her children is beginning to be recognized as more reality-based than that of Earth as an endless resource for human consumption. The metaphor of the natural world as a life-giving Mother is ancient, and it appears in many different cultures. Many indigenous cultures around the world refer to the Earth as Mother. This metaphor enshrines an archetypal recognition of the dependence of our bodies on the life-giving generosity of the Earth, as well as of our responsibility to enter into an intimate relationship of mutual caregiving. A revival of this story of physical interdependence and intimacy with the Earth fits well with the growing emergence of naturecentrism.

Commentators offer a few cautions, however. The metaphor of "Mother Earth" sometimes seems to place the Earth over against culture, creating a binary that fails to recognize how completely nature and culture are always-and-everywhere intertwined with one another. This binary of nature and culture, in turn, may be identified with the binary of female and male, thus reducing "feminine" nature to a more passive home-making role while the "men's work" of economics and politics is elevated to another plane that is not subject to the constraints of nature. Moreover, the Mother Earth metaphor may enshrine an assumption that nature's beneficence to humanity is unconditional and unstinting, like that of a perfectly loving mother. This releases "child" humankind from the necessity of recognizing limits in our use of the goods of nature. A further effect may be to contribute to the reduction of women's roles to that of motherhood, with the assumption that their duty of other-centered service is also unlimited.

In short, the old story of Mother Earth often colluded with some problematic stereotypes of motherhood, which in turn colluded with problematic philosophical and political ideologies. It is still a classic story, however, that bears a truth desperately needed in an era when humanity's relationship with the Earth is in major trouble. After exploring several other faces of the contemporary movement to resituate humankind within the community of Earth creatures, we will return to the question of how to refresh this old story for a new time.

Gaia theory

In view of some of the critiques of the Mother Earth image, a quite different way of envisioning Earth appears in James Lovelock's Gaia theory. In Greek mythology, Gaia (Earth) was a ferocious goddess who gave birth to many other powerful gods and goddesses. Rather than envisioning nature as a personified goddess figure, however, Lovelock argues that the combined natural ecosystemic processes of the entire Earth system function something like those of a living organism. Just as an organism self-regulates to maintain its optimum temperature range, chemical balance, nutrient and waste exchange, and so on, so does the Earth system as a whole. This is why the Earth has had a relatively benign, consistent climate for the entire eleven-thousand-year period (the geological epoch of the Holocene) during which humanity developed agriculture and civilization.

While Lovelock's theory gives Gaia the feminine name of the Greek Earth-goddess, he did not envision her as a beneficent divine mother but rather as a complex, all-encompassing set of biochemical processes that self-regulate so as to maintain the balances supportive of her participant communities of life. Gaia, as Lovelock presents her, is far from a tender, docile mother quietly pining for human love. Rather, she is a volatile, fierce, implacable force of nature who—at our current moment in geohistory—is on the verge of a terrifying rampage due to all the unbalancing forces humanity has added to the mix. The onslaught of disasters created by shifting global air and water flow, rising seas, hurricanes, heat waves, floods, ecosystem collapses, and so forth may appear shockingly impersonal or even cruel in its lack of concern for human well-being, but these are actually nothing more than Gaia's response to the effects of human activity during the "Great Acceleration" of fossil-fuel burning and other pollution during the last seventy-five years.

A definite plus for Gaia theory is that it is based in science rather than only in mythic or archetypal reflection. Prior to formulating the theory, James Lovelock underwent thorough training in chemistry and medicine, and he had already received high honors for his numerous discoveries and inventions. Another plus is that, rather than enshrining a nature/culture binary, this approach includes human cultural, economic, and political activities within the same category as other natural processes. Humans and our activities are in no way separate from nature; everything we do is part of nature and participates in how natural processes unfold, with impacts no different from those of any other "natural" creature or force. In addition, Gaia theory does not stereotype the feminine (and therefore women) as passive, benign, controllable, and always available to serve men.

Of course, this theory has also attracted critiques. It was strongly rejected by many mechanistically-minded scientists who felt that it went too far in giving Earth a name and a kind of "personality," as if Earth were literally a living super-organism. They were also deeply bothered by any hint of teleology, as if the Earth could have desire and intention to stay in balance. However, it is important to note that Lovelock does not say that the Earth *is* an organism, only that it is self-regulating in a similarly complex manner and that it responds as a whole interconnected system, not just as a jumble of parts.

According to Bruno Latour, in responding to his critics Lovelock does his best to thread the needle between too much "deanimation" and too much "overanimation."[3] The standard deanimating stance of the last few centuries of Western science reduces everything in the natural world to knowable and controllable parts without any agency of their own. Literally to call Earth a person or super-organism with intentions and arbitrary moods, on the other hand, would be to overanimate it. Lovelock strives to identify a middle ground in which the complex interconnecting activity of billions of living agents cocreates a whole Earth system that in no way can be called "inanimate," even though it also cannot, strictly speaking, be called an organism.

A second critique of Gaia theory is that it may employ outdated ecological assumptions about organismic and ecosystemic homeostasis. Some of the more recent research suggests that change and imbalance are more pervasive in ecosystems than previously assumed. In the natural world, organisms eventually die, and ecosystems do not remain the same for long. In this view, Gaia theory is overly optimistic in depicting an Earth that has maintained its thermal and biochemical balance over many millennia and could have continued to do so

---

3. Bruno Latour, *Facing Gaia: Eight Lectures on the New Climatic Regime*, ed. Catherine Porter (Cambridge, UK: Polity, 2017), 86–100.

if not for human-caused pollution. The worry is that this optimism gives some commentators an excuse to assume that somehow the Earth will "save" us from our current ecological crisis by finding a way to come back to its Holocene balance.

However, Lovelock never said that Earth could maintain its traditional, human-life-supporting balance no matter what was thrown at it by human activity. Over his long career he became increasingly pessimistic about the immediate future of Earth as a habitat for human beings. In fact, he affirmed that the Earth is now inexorably set on the path of a long, volatile, unpredictable search for completely new balances as it reacts to the onslaught of skyrocketing carbon, multiple forms of chemical pollution, the massive destruction of ecosystems, and widespread extinctions. There is no guarantee that the Earth that emerges from this search will be supportive of human life.

The new animism

As the Earth begins its search for its next balance of being, humans too are searching for how to live through this next, extraordinarily difficult period when the comforting consistency of the Holocene climate will be long gone. In this context, elements of the ancient animistic worldview that was once regarded as "primitive" are re-emerging as a viable alternative to modern dualism. This "new animism" affirms that life and interpersonal relationship connect every creature and being on Earth (and beyond). Even Pope Francis has written of all creatures as our neighbors and kin who are tenderly loved by God, and of our intimate connection to geographies and landscapes.[4]

---

4. Pope Francis, *On Care for Our Common Home: Laudato Si'* (Washington, DC: United States Conference of Catholic Bishops, 2015).

The term "animism" first came to prominence within the academic discipline of anthropology, and today it is anthropologists who are among those proposing that this term that has been much disparaged can find new life in a postmodern world. This requires first understanding why animism is a problematic term, then considering its potential for significant reframing. The term was originally coined by the vitalist chemist and philosopher Georg Stahl (1679–1734). It was made famous, however, by pioneering anthropologist E. B. Tylor in his 1871 book *Primitive Culture*. The religions of so-called primitive peoples, according to Tylor, were centered around beliefs in non-empirical "souls" or "spirits" existing in animals, plants, landscape features, heavenly bodies, and so on. He wanted to call this "spiritualism" but, since that term had already been claimed with a different meaning, he chose Stahl's "animism" instead.[5] In his view, animism was a foundational form of human religion that has been naturally superseded by more mature and reality-based forms as civilization has developed.

Tylor's theory is based on several problematic assumptions. The first of these, obviously, is that the religious intuitions of indigenous peoples are primitive, immature, and, frankly, just plain wrong. A second problematic assumption is defining indigenous spiritual experience in the thoroughly Western and modern dualistic terms of (non-empirical) "spirit" vs. (empirical) "matter." As we will see, this assumption goes to the very root of what is so much in need of re-thinking today. Finally, it is problematic to describe these indigenous intuitions as "beliefs." The focus of indigenous

5. Martin D. Stringer, "Building on Belief: Defining Animism in Tylor and Contemporary Society," in *The Handbook of Contemporary Animism*, ed. Graham Harvey (London: Routledge, 2015), 64.

spirituality is generally on immersion in the flow of lived experience and the search for practical benefit, whereas in Tylor's Western context, a belief would be understood as a fixed statement of cognitive truth.

In the 150 years since Tylor's publication, many anthropologists who have engaged in intensive fieldwork among indigenous peoples have strongly reacted against use of the term "animism." They identify it as a pejorative misnaming that was imposed on indigenous peoples in the context of the colonial project of dominating and disappropriating them. In this view, the term does more to obscure than to enlighten the actual character of indigenous spiritualities. Thus, it is somewhat controversial to have it revived in the movement of "the new animism." Nonetheless, at this time a postmodern reframing of animism is engendering serious discussion in the field of anthropology and beyond.

This "new animism" has two main faces. One face is a thorough, fieldwork-based re-evaluation of indigenous spiritualities in order to understand better the vast diversity of ways in which their participants experientially engage in living, dynamic relationships with the creatures and features among whom they live. While no generalization can completely encompass all indigenous cultures, the gist of the research findings seems to be that indigenous communities whose survival depends on intimate daily participation in their local ecosystem develop ritualized customs of communication with the creatures and landscape features with which they are interdependent. This communication presumes a certain mutuality between human and other living and non-living beings, at least some of which are experienced as persons like ourselves who are able to understand, communicate, and respond with intelligence and ethical behavior. In general, the goal of such communication is to maintain as harmonious as possible relationships with all, including those with whom one is involved as predator, prey, and/or competitor.

The second face of the new animism, and the only one that I am at all qualified to engage in, is the proposal of a postmodern animism that is observed to be emerging among the denizens of the postmodern Western world, especially those most aware of the depth of the current ecological crisis. This version of new animism does not claim to be based on any specific indigenous spirituality, and in fact it is in many ways quite different from any of them. At the same time, it is deeply respectful of indigenous peoples and eager to walk beside them as co-learners and co-activists in hope of seeding a better future than the one that is currently bearing down upon us. Learning from indigenous peoples, as Priscilla Stuckey notes, need not involve a dominating form of appropriation; rather, it may be "not for [our] gain but for loss—for the loss of stable meanings and of foundations that once appeared secure."[6]

My Octopus Teacher

A popularized example of this new animism is the movie *My Octopus Teacher*. The film tells the story of a depressed and burned-out filmmaker who retreats to spend a year snorkeling in the waters of False Bay, South Africa, where he had spent his childhood. The gist of the story is the astonishing friendship that he develops through daily underwater visits with a female common octopus. Also astonishing is the level of intelligence and adaptability demonstrated by this relatively small mollusk. Mollusks are on a quite different branch of the evolutionary tree from humans, so observing this high a level of intelligence,

---

6. Priscilla Stuckey, "The Animal versus the Social: Rethinking Individual and Community in Western Cosmology," in *The Handbook of Contemporary Animism*, ed. Graham Harvey (London: Routledge, 2015), 191.

creativity, and apparent affective bonding is revelatory of the potential for human relationship with any living creature. The movie presents the experience of this relationship as deeply healing for the human protagonist, and seemingly at least enjoyable for the octopus. Many viewers have found the movie not only fascinating but also deeply reassuring as it offers a hopeful vision of vital, mutually enriching human-creature relationships.

Not surprisingly, there are many commentaries on the internet that express doubt about whether such a relationship between a human and a mollusk could have happened as depicted. They point out that we as humans have no access to what the octopus is feeling or cognizing, and so both filmmaker and viewers are inevitably anthropomorphizing a creature that is in so many ways profoundly different from us. Their view would be that the human protagonist is simply projecting an imaginary relationship onto the world of nature.

The new animism, however, makes different assumptions about this scenario. First, it presumes no hierarchy of creatures in which humans are in a different and superior category. Humans, octopuses, and all others have different skills and capacities, but ontologically they are all equal and all interdependent. Second, the fundamental sameness of all creatures is that they are actively engaging in a multitude of relationships with the world around them in order to survive and thrive—which includes simply enjoying life.[7] Of course humans are anthropomorphizing, and the octopus is undoubtedly "octopusizing." That does not prevent the two from engaging with each other with curiosity and creativity—and discovering something in the relationship that each needs or enjoys. Third,

---

7. Tim Ingold, *The Perception of the Environment* (New York: Routledge, 2021).

imagination is not an illusion concocted in the human mind to distort the "real world"; rather, it is an embedded tool for guiding and enhancing engagement with the world.[8] Imagining friendship with the octopus guides friendly interactions. Telling the story of the friendship, as in the movie, guides viewers into living similar stories themselves. The participatory delight and healing that is being co-created is as real, if not more so, as the "objective" character of what is going on.

The new animism, then, arises as a recognition of the failure of the fundamental Western assumption that human life will be improved by the maximum application of our objectifying capabilities channeled into technological manipulation of the physical world, which is envisioned as ontologically inferior to humans and always available to serve immediate human needs. The new animism is not necessarily a wholesale rejection of all science and technology, but it does call for placing these within a completely different set of basic assumptions. Humans are participants in a living Earth community peopled by tens of thousands of interdependent species and ecosystemic dynamics. Human life is sustainable in the long term only by developing skills of embodied collaboration in mutually beneficial relationships with all other participants in the Earth community. This requires learning to respect, listen to, and communicate with other-than-human persons.

Living in the kindom

"The kingdom of God is in your midst" is a phrase that is at the very core of Jesus's preaching. Thirty years ago, feminist the-

---

8. Tim Ingold, "Dreaming of Dragons: On the Imagination of Real Life," *The Journal of the Royal Anthropological Institute* 19, no. 4 (2013): 734–52, https://doi.org/10.1111/1467-9655.12062.

ologians had the insight that a more conducive image for our time would be, "The kin-dom of God is in your midst!" They argued that this is not just clever wordplay, but actually a more accurate interpretation of what Jesus was intending to convey. The biblical image of God as king has deep roots in the Hebrew Bible, and it built on the lived experience of ancient Semites who lived under monarchical governments. The typical king of the time was a highly authoritarian male leader who commanded imperiously from the top of a hierarchical structure. Jesus, however, did not portray his own leadership as anything like that. He was a humble servant-leader who walked among the people, washed feet, and fed his disciples with his own body and blood. His embodiment of the kingdom of God subverted the oppressive, hierarchical model of kingship that people of the time were familiar with.

Fast-forwarding to the twenty-first century, authoritarian monarchy is no longer a commonly experienced form of government. Meanwhile, humanity is entering into a period of crisis in which the last thing needed is to encourage authoritarianism, oppression, and hierarchy. As noted above, the call of our era is for humanity to rediscover our roots in the humus of Earth and our kinship with all the other creatures of the Earth. The "kin-dom of God" articulates this. The claim of this book is that it is, in fact, what Jesus preaches to us today.

The idea that all creatures on Earth are our kin can sound, at first, like a rather mushy-minded concept suitable to be embraced only by those with heads in the clouds. It turns out, however, that it is actually hard science.[9] Microbial life began on planet Earth about four billion years ago, and every

---

9. Lynn Margulis and Dorion Sagan, *Microcosmos: Four Billion Years of Evolution from Our Microbial Ancestors* (Berkeley: University of California Press, 1997).

form of life since then—whether bacterial, fungal, plant, or animal—descends from that original ancestor. This means that every living creature that exists now on planet Earth, or ever existed, is literally our "cousin." It is true that in most cases the relation is distant, amounting to being a cousin several thousand (or hundred thousand) times removed. It is nonetheless of supreme significance to understand that we really are all in this together. All life on Earth derives from the same ancestry, shares variations of the same DNA, and depends for viability on the same biochemical processes that were worked out in the first two billion years by our tiny microbial ancestors. As a biological species, humans are not any more special or climactic than any other species. We are simply one small, late-arriving, and precarious branch on a tree of life richly tangled with millions of other branches, many far more venerable than our own.

This brings us back to the humility of realizing that we humans are creatures born of humus, just like every other Earth creature. Humility, human, and humus are all words derived from the same root, meaning "soil." When Genesis 2:7 says, "The Lord God formed the human being from the dust of the earth," it reveals a kind of eucharistic dynamic (with a small e) built into our very existence. On Ash Wednesday when we hear the words, "Dust you are, and to dust you shall return," they may give us a little shiver of dread as they remind us of our inevitable death. But they are also a reminder of how profoundly we are interconnected with the community of life on Earth. This humus from which humans are made consists of the decomposed bodies of all creatures who ever lived. It teems with trillions of microbes and tiny creatures, as well as fragments of millions of rocks and minerals from a multitude of times and places. All these have given their lives for us—and one day, when our own bodies decompose, we will give our lives for them. The cycle of "dust to dust" is, fundamentally, a radical sharing of life.

Symbiosis and new life

The science of our shared community with other Earth creatures is found not only in the evolution of our DNA but also in the intimacy of our coexistence with the billions of microbes that live in, on, and around us.[10] As the ability to detect and classify microbial life has exploded in recent decades, scientists have confirmed the shocking fact that microbes are, literally, everywhere. The air we breathe, the food we eat, every part of our homes and offices, and everything else that we encounter is both permeated and coated with invisible living creatures. After spending decades devising ever more sophisticated techniques to rid our constructed worlds of "germs," the realization is dawning that the vast majority of microbial life in our environments does no damage to our well-being, and that much of it participates in functions that have beneficial effects for ourselves and other living creatures. This does not mean that we can let our guard down about locating and counteracting the small number of microbes that actually are dangerous to us, but it does mean that we need a far more targeted approach.

Within our own bodies, microbes outnumber our own cells while making up about ten percent of our body weight. Our digestive processes depend on the participation of many species of bacteria, to the point that physicians today are concerned that the declining biodiversity in modern human digestive tracts may be contributing to many forms of ill health. Meanwhile,

---

10. Ed Yong, *I Contain Multitudes: The Microbes within Us and a Grander View of Life* (Ecco—an imprint of HarperCollins Publishers, 2016).

millions of bacteria, fungi, and viruses from as many as one thousand different species inhabit our skin and bodily orifices, each species specializing in a different region or function. Despite the "ick" factor that many experience on hearing this, these symbiotic relationships have been active as long as the human species has existed, and they are deeply woven into nature's ways of keeping us healthy. A healthy body, in its natural state, is not one freed from all other creatures, but rather a thriving and balanced symbiotic community of creatures that work together to perform the functions necessary to maintain the life and vitality of all community participants.

All this contributes to a major philosophical shift from regarding things as separate individuals to regarding them as dynamically emergent within a multitude of relationships. The work of biologist Lynn Margulis on the significance of symbiosis corroborates this. Her most important research discovery was that leaps in evolution often take place more by symbiosis —that is, different species living in such intimate interdependence that boundaries loosen and genetic material is exchanged—than by Darwin's "natural selection."[11] This is particularly true on the level of bacteria, which exchange DNA so easily that, she says, they essentially have access to "a single gene pool and hence to the adaptive mechanisms of the entire bacterial kingdom."[12] Her work showed that some of the major steps forward in evolution came when bacteria that were originally symbiotes literally became incorporated into larger bodies. This is the origin, for example, of the mitochondria that fuel every cell in our bodies, as well as the cilia found in sperm, ears, lungs, the digestive tract, and elsewhere.

---

11. Lynn Margulis, *Symbiotic Planet: A New Look at Evolution, Science Masters* (New York: Basic Books, 1998).

12. Margulis and Sagan, *Microcosmos*, 16.

To be sure, natural selection does occur. A recent example is research showing that since humans have been using sweet poisons to kill cockroaches, many cockroaches are no longer attracted by sweet food. This has changed their mating process, since the sweet treat that males used to offer the females before copulation is no longer effective. Instead, males move more swiftly and firmly to accomplish the deed before the female can depart.[13] Still, this is a minor shift within the habits of a species, as compared to a major leap forward such as discovering a whole new way to convert energy to fuel (as occurred with the evolution of mitochondria). The significance of Margulis's discovery is that rather than placing a competitive dynamic at the center of life's development—"survival of the fittest," for example—it places interspecies collaboration at the center. It is when species get intimate with one another that something truly new arises.

As was the case with Lovelock, Margulis's proposals about the centrality of symbiosis were so revolutionary that they were initially rejected by most of her scientific peers. Once her research discoveries were proven, however, she received recognition as a uniquely gifted scientist. Showing characteristic courage, Margulis spent several years collaborating with Lovelock in developing the Gaia hypothesis despite the fact that this also led to severe attacks on her scientific reputation. While Lovelock's focus was on the mechanisms that sustain Gaia's homeostasis, Margulis's interest was in Gaia as a holistic being integrating the lives and functions of all her participants—in other words, another example of symbiosis.[14]

---

13. "Bittersweet: Bait-Averse Cockroaches Shudder at Sugar," *Science Daily*, May 23, 2013, https://www.sciencedaily.com/releases/2013/05/130523142959.htm.

14. Michael Ruse, *The Gaia Hypothesis: Science on a Pagan Planet* (Chicago: The University of Chicago Press, 2013), chap. 7.

Conclusion

This chapter has spelled out the problem of the Earth-separated life, as well as a variety of efforts to rediscover and reclaim humanity's physical and spiritual implication within the web of life on Earth. As we consider whether the story of Mother Earth can be renovated for this purpose, one helpful approach may be to reflect on how the trajectory of life gives each of us a variety of experiences that contribute to how we imagine the Earth as "motherly." Before we are born, our mother carries us in her womb; she encompasses us completely and provides for our every need, without us even being aware or taking any initiative. During childhood, we radically depend upon our mother and rather imperiously demand her tender care, even as gradually we learn to recognize her and her needs as separate from ourselves. In adolescence our mother may become our adversary, with whom our interests and desires heatedly clash. When we reach adulthood, we discover her as an enjoyable companion. As she enters her final years, we may need to care for our mother as she cared for us as a child.

Only by including this whole relational trajectory can we arrive at a viable story of "Mother Earth" for today. We are indeed born of the Earth, utterly dependent on her, and we often instinctively behave like children who expect her always to unstintingly provide for our every need. Yet we also find some of Earth's ways alien, frustrating, or harsh—and this aspect of our daily experience will become ever more prominent as she reacts to our self-centeredness with the fury of wind, water, fire, and plague. Still, on good days we can delight in just spending time relaxing and enjoying Earth's presence. Sooner or later, though, the days arrive when we must learn the necessity of laboring on her behalf, no longer making our own enjoyment the main priority. The new story of Mother Earth must encompass all of this, rather than reducing her motherhood only to that experienced by the infant or the child. In the updated story of Mother Earth, humanity must be both humble child and mature adult, able both to receive and give with tenderhearted mutuality.

REFLECTION QUESTIONS:

What is your most profound memory of connection with the natural world or with a wild creature? Journal about this memory and what it might be calling you to today.

How does the image of "Mother Earth" resonate with you? What about the "Gaia" image? Do you have another favorite image of the Earth and its role in your life?

FOR FURTHER READING:

Trevor Bechtel, Matt Eaton, and Tim Harvie, *Encountering Earth: Thinking Theologically with a More-Than-Human World* (Eugene, OR: Cascade, 2018).

Shawn Sanford Beck, *Christian Animism* (Christian Alternative, 2015).

Daniel G. Deffenbaugh, *Learning the Language of the Fields: Tilling and Keeping as Christian Vocation* (Cambridge, MA: Cowley, 2006).

Pope Francis, *On Care for Our Common Home: Laudato Si'* (Washington, DC: United States Conference of Catholic Bishops, 2015).

4

THE EMERGING HEART

The previous chapter described how the growing movement of naturecentrism eschews any gap between body and spirit, or between nature and culture. In view of that, we asserted that Jesus's core preaching of the "kingdom of God" can be more appropriately formulated today as the "kin-dom of God," bringing humans back to the humility of being simple members and servants of the community of Earth creatures. This new perspective demands a thorough reformulation of our understanding of Jesus, what it means to identify him as "Christ" and as the second person of the Holy Trinity, and his role in relation to humans and other creatures.

In this chapter, I will begin by exploring how Christ has always been alive and active in creation, even before the historical birth of Jesus. It may seem surprising to begin with what is often referred to as the "preexistence of Christ," since in recent decades it has been more common to begin Christological reflection with focus on the human life and preaching of Jesus. A major reason for this preference for "Christology from below" is that for several centuries before the Second Vatican Council (1962–1965), the portrayal of Christ in regal divine glory had tended to eclipse awareness of his earthy humanity. In addition, people today are generally oriented to a more empirical, fact-based style of thinking. While Jesus was an identifiable human being who lived in Israel in the first century CE, for many of our contemporaries the concept of the preexistent Christ appears more like an airy construct built out of little more than textual allusions and theological assumptions. The idea of a God-man sent "down" from heaven above simply no longer fits with our everyday worldview. With reformulation, however, the preexistence of Christ can find new meaning within our more science-based perspective.

A sketch of an evolutionary Christology

While ancient peoples had a variety of cosmologies, the predominant ones in the European-influenced regions envisioned the Earth as the center of the universe. Even after that was debunked by such luminaries as Copernicus and Galileo, it took centuries to discover the truly mind-boggling vastness of a cosmos in which the Earth is barely a tiny dot. Another "new idea" that is taking time to absorb theologically is evolution. Until about a century and a half ago, people generally assumed that each creature had been created looking and behaving just as we see it today. The discovery of the long, intricate, and interwoven genealogies of all living species reveals, as we have seen, that calling insects, worms and bacteria "kin" is not just a fuzzy metaphor; it is fact-based.

Thus, the scientific revolutions of the past century and a half demand that we think very differently about Christ. What if Christ has been concretely, physically active since the beginning of creation, at work in all the evolutionary processes of the universe? In that case, in and through those processes, God is step by step bringing the fullness of the "kin-dom of

God" into existence. These processes appear to us as wild, tangled, often terrifying, yet also gloriously beautiful and astoundingly creative. Jesus's arrival on Earth two thousand years ago was not the beginning of the Incarnation, but a decisive step forward in its fulfillment. Yet Christ's mission to make the Earth a true "kin-dom" fully enlivened by his Heart still remains incomplete, calling upon us to participate in bringing it about.

This simplified sketch of an evolutionary Christology will be filled out in the pages that follow. Our particular focus will be on the slow, often obscure emergence of the quality of "heart," culminating in what we today know as the Sacred Heart of Jesus. A question that will certainly need to be attended to is whether this evolutionary view is too optimistic, especially considering the current grim assessments of what human activity is doing to the Earth's future viability as a habitat for humans (not to mention thousands of other threatened species). We must never forget that Jesus's earthly life did not end in triumph, but on the cross with the lifeblood pouring from his pierced heart. This too must be accounted for in an evolutionary Christology.

Heart as cosmic interiority

In chapter 1 I wrote about the heart as having four functions in human life: interiority, bonding, belonging, and meaning. To sum them all up, the heart is an interior space of loving embrace. The interiority of the heart is not mere aloneness, but the capacity to know oneself as a space where the depth of love dwells. This space opens to embrace and be embraced by others when one bonds with another, commits to belonging to a group, or reaches out to engage in meaningful activity. When we say that the quality of "heart" emerges only gradually in creation, we refer to this capacity to dwell in the fullness of love, to embrace all creatures as kin, and to act intentionally so as to create a world fully enlivened by heartfulness.

Scientists estimate that the universe is thirteen and a half billion years old, and that planet Earth has existed for about four and a half billion of those years. While we can posit that the quality of heart exists "from the beginning" in God, it emerges in the created world only gradually over all those billions of years. With an evolutionary understanding of creation, we can envision the created world experimenting throughout these eons with how to build creatures who can manifest the heartful interiority of God. In some way, every creature is such an experiment. In a recent book, marine scientist and photographer Gaelin Rosenwaks recounts in detail the complex, lifelong relationships of mutual affection among whale family members, especially the females. She notes that sperm whale groups in different parts of the world "vary in behavior and can be distinguished by their language, traditions and codas." She then describes spending half an hour completely captivated in a tender mutual gaze with one of the whales. "There is nothing like looking into the eye of a sperm whale," she says. "Their eyes are filled with wisdom that penetrates your soul."[1]

This and other descriptions of a high level of "heart qualities" such as complex relationships, fidelity, culture, affection, and wisdom among animals is surprising if one assumes that these qualities are reserved exclusively, or at least primarily, for members of the human species. On the other hand, if one accepts the concept of an evolving universe heading toward the fullest manifestation of heartfulness, it makes sense that what is seeking to emerge will appear in a vast array of different degrees and forms. The more we learn about life on Earth, the more we discover this kind of universe.

---

1. Gaelin Rosenwaks, *Sperm Whales: The Gentle Goliaths of the Oceans*, 1st U.S. edition (New York: Rizzoli International Publications, Inc., 2022).

Evolution and emergence

In the study of evolution, Darwin's principle of natural selection has typically been regarded as sacrosanct. This principle states that when random genetic variations or mutations occur, some will confer a survival and reproduction advantage and so these will increase in the population. This accounts well for gradual evolution of greater fitness within a species, as well as for the development of a range of closely related species, for example, the many different types of canids (dog-like species). It accounts less well for the emergence of significantly new forms of organization or levels of complexity, for example, the move from single-celled to multicellular life, or from reptiles to mammals. As noted in a previous chapter, newer theories of evolution such as that of Lynn Margulis propose that symbiotic relationships and exchange of DNA at the microbial level are also major contributing factors that can help to account for some of these more surprising and unpredictable emergences.

The concept of emergence is a way of describing what happens when a new level of complexity comes forth that could not have been predicted from observing the prior interaction of the components that contribute to it. In other words, one cannot trace a straightforward causal chain that brings about the new phenomenon. The concept became prominent in the early to mid-twentieth century as scientists began to realize that systems with enormous numbers of moving and interacting parts exceed the capacities of linear calculation, even with the most advanced computers. The novel structures that can emerge from such systems are in principle unpredictable. The most outstanding examples are the emergence of the universe, the emergence of life, and the emergence of mind. However, this principle also operates in many natural systems and throughout all of evolution.

A major debate is whether emergence operates in a "weak" or "strong" manner. Those who affirm only weak emergence believe that eventually the causal lineage could be teased out by the advance of science. In this view, emergence is a kind of stopgap concept to identify phenomena that are not yet fully understood, but probably will be eventually. Proponents of strong emergence, on the other hand, argue that since emergence is based in the science of chaos and complexity, it involves an ineradicable element of unpredictability. Chaotic systems are those in which the movement of component parts (for example, air molecules) is completely random. Yet the study of such systems reveals that complex patterns (hurricanes, tornadoes) emerge out of randomness. That hurricanes and tornadoes will emerge can be predicted, but exactly where and when cannot be determined until the patterns actually begin to manifest themselves.

When theologians take up these concepts of evolution and emergence, a key question is that of whether evolution has a direction or, alternatively, is completely random. An oversimplified, but common, sketch of the evolutionary tree makes it appear as a more or less straight line from the simplicity of one-celled microbes to the complexity of human beings, who are placed at the "top" of the tree. Such a picture often makes it appear that from the beginning, the purpose of each step of evolution was to eventually create human beings. This picture fits well with modern ideas about "progress," as well as with a naively anthropocentric theology.

Scientists, however, disagree strongly with this picture. They point out that any creature alive today could be placed at the "top" of such an evolutionary tree and presumed to be its intended result, since every creature (whether microbe, algae, fungi, plant, or animal) has an equally long lineage extending back to the origin of life on Earth. Rather than being like a tree shooting upward, evolution proceeds in a very messy tangle going out in all directions from the origin of life. In fact, most of its branches go nowhere; 99 percent of all species that have ever existed on Earth are now extinct. The verdict is still out on whether modern *Homo sapiens*, whose mere 300,000 years of existence makes us still a very young species, will soon join the 99 percent.

Even if one rejects naïve anthropocentrism—that is, the idea that the purpose of evolution has been to create *Homo sapiens*—the question of whether evolution has a direction still remains. It seems self-evident that evolution inclines toward increasing biodiversity, since life on Earth began at some point with one species and now has produced as many as one trillion species. If nothing else, the evolutionary process is wildly and gloriously experimental, trying out vast numbers of configurations of life. It also appears that evolution demonstrates a clear trend toward the emergence of increasingly complex, sensitive, and intelligent creatures. Even though not every instance of change or every new species follows this trend, it can be traced repeatedly on different branches of evolution, resulting in an expansive array of creatures manifesting startlingly various capabilities of perception, motility, relationality, and intelligence.

Does *Homo sapiens* represent the emergence of a new level of complexity, sensitivity, and intelligence, beyond that of any other living creature? Although to many the answer might be self-evidently "Yes," this too is a debated question. Zoological research confirms that our native capacities in the areas of perception and social organization are exceeded by those of many other species.[2] Where we clearly excel is in the construction of tools that assist our manipulation of the environment to suit our purposes. Yet it remains to be seen whether this is a sus-

---

2. Ed Yong, *An Immense World: How Animal Senses Reveal the Hidden Realms around Us* (New York: Random House, 2022).

tainable variation of intelligence, in view of the mounting evidence of environmental destruction as a result of human technological "advances."

Teilhard de Chardin and evolutionary theology

The previous section provided an overview of scientific consensus (and some debated issues) regarding evolution and emergence. The present project, however, is a work of theology and spirituality, not science. It has only been about one hundred years since the Jesuit paleontologist Pierre Teilhard de Chardin began to develop the first thoroughgoing Christian theology of evolution. At the time, his ideas about bringing God down from a supernatural heaven into the ever-changing realm of stars, volcanoes, rocks, amoeba, and animals were so shocking that his superiors regarded them as most likely heretical. On that basis, most of his writings were suppressed until after his death. They began to be better known only in the late 1950s and '60s, and soon they began to evoke widespread excitement among many members of the reading public as well as some theologians.

Thomas King observes that while as a youth Teilhard may have tended toward a materialist pantheism (in which God is diffused in all matter), as his mature thought emerged he became a spiritual pantheist (in which God is the form of all matter).[3] In the latter, it is the Heart of Christ, the Omega Point, that draws matter to be formed more and more to itself through all the complex processes of evolution. As Teilhard put it:

> [Christ] is no longer master of the world solely because he
> has been proclaimed to be such, but because he animates the

---

3. Thomas M. King, *Teilhard's Mysticism of Knowing* (New York: Seabury Press, 1981), 14–15.

whole range of things from top to bottom; a Christ who dominates the history of heaven and earth not solely because they have been given to him, but because his gestation, his birth and gradual consummation constitute physically the only definitive reality in which the evolution of the world is expressed.[4]

A more controversial part of Teilhard's thought was that the next stage in human development would be the emergence of a "noosphere" or collective of human minds organized into a kind of superorganism. Some critics interpret this as an effort to lift the human species above and away from its roots in the Earth community. Writing mainly before the "great acceleration" of industrialization after World War II that has so severely damaged the Earth ecosystem, Teilhard was often uncritically optimistic about the potential of science and technology to guide the perfection of the human species and the Earth. He, as well as some of his disciples, have also been accused of being "ecomodernists" who are too quick to believe that technological progress can make short work of any problems (such as global climate change) and quickly raise humanity to a completely new level of consciousness and ease of life. Thus, there is plenty to critique about Teilhard's ideas. While claims that he was racist have been debunked,[5] it can be argued that his unabashed anthropocentrism and enthusiasm for the technologization of the Earth remain problematic.

---

4. Pierre Teilhard de Chardin, "Christology and Evolution," in *Christianity and Evolution*, trans. René Hague (New York: Harcourt, 1974), 89.

5. John P. Slattery, "Pierre Teilhard de Chardin's Legacy of Eugenics and Racism Can't Be Ignored," *Religion Dispatches*, May 2018; John F. Haught, "Trashing Teilhard: How Not to Read a Great Religious Thinker," *Commonweal*, February 19, 2019, https://www.commonwealmagazine.org/trashing-teilhard.

Despite all this, Teilhard must be given credit as the genius who recognized that twentieth-century theology would have to change profoundly in order to preach the gospel to people whose mentality is shaped by the findings of modern science. As Franciscan sister and theologian Ilia Delio puts it, "The most fundamental shift in our understanding of the cosmos is the move from the vision of a universe launched essentially in its present form by the hand of the creator at the beginning of time to a vision of the cosmos as a dynamic, unfolding chemical process, immensely large in both time and space." In this universe, she continues, the human being is not the center but "the growing tip of an evolutionary trend."[6] It was Teilhard who had the courage and the vision to sketch out a first draft of a theology that could fully embrace that shift. He also offered a spiritual vision that has given many hope and enthusiasm to work for a better world.

Many theologians of his time (and since) dismissed Teilhard's proposals because he lacked full professional training in theology and wrote in a style that often relied more on rhetorical flourish than on careful footnotes. Similarly, Thomas Berry (1914–2009), a Passionist priest whose lectures and writings on the urgent need for humanity to reclaim its Earth-rootedness have inspired so many, had a doctorate in European intellectual history rather than in theology. In recent decades, however, so many well-prepared theologians have taken up the mantle of evolutionary theology that it would be impossible to name them all. Among Catholics, some of the more prominent have been Karl Rahner, John Haught, Ilia Delio, Celia Deane-Drummond, Denis Edwards, and Elizabeth A. Johnson. Protestants include Jürgen Moltmann, Sally McFague, Catherine Keller, Ted Peters, Holmes Rolston III, and Jay McDaniels, among many others.

---

6. Ilia Delio, *Christ in Evolution* (Maryknoll, NY: Orbis Books, 2008), 21.

Ecological and evolutionary theology received a strong papal endorsement in 2015 when Pope Francis issued his encyclical *Laudato Si'* and again in 2023 with *Laudate Deum*. All these theologians are developing variations of the idea that evolution is the way divine creativity continues to work its way out in created matter, bringing forth the kind of world God desires.

A theological manifesto

Rather than review all the different approaches currently on offer, at this point I will simply sketch out the approach to evolutionary theology that I am embracing in this project. A basic principle is that science must be thoroughly respected at the same time that God must not be reduced to only what can be known by science. In line with nearly all contemporary theologies, I reject the concept of an interventionist God who reaches into the created world to accomplish things apart from natural processes. A theological analysis, then, has to go beyond science-based knowledge to account for the presence and action of God, yet without disregarding or contradicting the legitimate findings of science. For a helpful perspective on how to do that, I turn to the approach of Arthur Peacocke (1924–2006), who was both an Anglican priest and a biochemist.

Peacocke took the position that God acts not by directly influencing any of the parts of creation, but by active embrace of the created universe as a whole. This is another way of saying that although God does not interfere with or manipulate any of the natural causal chains that make things happen, God's will is always and everywhere at work simply because of God's holistic presence to the whole of creation. This is how Peacocke put it:

> By analogy with the operation of whole-part influence in natural systems, [I suggest] that, because the "ontological gap(s)" between the world and God is/are located simply

everywhere in space and time, God could affect holistically the state of the world (the whole in this context) at all levels. Understood in this way, the proposal implies that patterns of events at the physical, biological, human, and even social levels could be influenced by divine intention without abrogating natural regularities at any of these levels.[7]

In regard to evolution and emergence, what this means is that divine intentionality gives direction to the process as a whole, yet God does not manipulate the process so that it will produce any specific species—say, kangaroos, or cockroaches, or *Homo sapiens*. All the scientifically described elements of random mutations, "survival of the fittest," breakthrough symbioses, tragic extinctions, and so on operate according to their own laws as part of the vast, wild, fecund, never-ending experimentation that continually boils forth new forms of life, and often just as quickly disposes of them.

The position taken here, in short, is that there is a divinely given direction to evolution, and that it is toward the emergence of creatures capable of manifesting qualities like those of the divine Heart. However, this is accomplished not by a straightforward process of increasingly complex construction by a so-called intelligent designer, but rather by a built-in process of constant experimentation with all the possibilities of created matter to see what comes forth and thrives. Embodying the quality of heart does in some sense confer an evolutionary advantage, because it involves increase in such capacities as alertness, intelligence, integrity, foresight, relationship-building, and loyalty. This is why, over time, the trend of evolution is

---

7. Arthur Peacocke, "Emergence, Mind and Divine Action: The Hierarchy of the Sciences in Relation to the Human Mind-Brain-Body," in *The Re-Emergence of Emergence: The Emergentist Hypothesis from Science to Religion*, ed. Philip Clayton and Paul Davies (Oxford: Oxford University Press, 2009), 275.

toward creatures with more of this quality. Nonetheless, creatures exhibiting this quality are by no means exempt from any of the painful exigencies of all life on Earth; on the contrary, they suffer these with even greater intensity and poignancy. The process of evolution is inevitably messy, wasteful, and tragic at the same time that it is stupendously creative and beautiful. This paradox is one of the meanings of the cross of Christ as the core symbol of Christianity.

The position I am taking is different from that of the eco-modernists who, as Clive Hamilton puts it, "focus on the marvelous ability of the human species to transcend any obstacle and continue its inexorable rise to a golden future."[8] The human species does indeed have some marvelous abilities, as seen in our astonishing technological feats in fields such as computer science, medicine, and space exploration. It remains to be seen, however, whether as a species we can muster enough heart to truly understand, accept, and behave responsibly in relation to our actual reality as just one more humble species in an interdependent community of living beings on a fragile planet. As Bruno Latour puts it, in the Holocene epoch beginning 11,000 years ago and culminating in modernity, humans set themselves the project of transcending Earth. In the Anthropocene that begins now, we must rediscover ourselves as "earthbound" and severely limited by what our terrestrial habitat can bear.[9] Failing to do so is likely to result in the end of the *Homo sapiens* experiment—or, if one is more optimistic, its reduction to a wisp of its former glory.

This is a grim assessment. Yet I do not propose to leave us foundering in anxiety and despair. The spiritual challenge we

---

8. Clive Hamilton, *Defiant Earth: The Fate of Humans in the Anthropocene* (Malden, MA: Polity, 2017), 59.

9. Bruno Latour, *Facing Gaia: Eight Lectures on the New Climatic Regime*, ed. Catherine Porter (Cambridge, UK: Polity, 2017), 248.

face is how to live with integrity, meaning, and genuine hope in such a perilous moment. The theological vision proposed here suggests that the answer is to discover and develop in fullness the qualities of heart that the created universe is intended to bring forth.

The emerging Heart

In this section I will briefly sketch the evolution of the universe and of life as the story of the emerging Heart at the heart of the world. As a scientific guide I have chosen biophysicist Harold J. Morowitz's *The Emergence of Everything*,[10] although for the sake of conciseness I have reduced his twenty-eight emergences to eight. While I do my best to follow what has been learned scientifically about these developments, this is a theological and spiritual account rather than, strictly speaking, a scientific one. I invite readers to keep in mind that when I say that a newly emerging development is being guided by the divine Heart, I do not intend this in an interventionist sense, as if the divine Heart were outside the process and manipulating it. Rather, the divine Heart both embraces the whole and lives within it, delighting in the ongoing creation of a world in its image.

1. *The emergence of the universe.* The most commonly accepted theory of the origin of our universe is that of the "Big Bang" taking place thirteen and a half billion years ago. This theory postulates that in the beginning, everything in the universe was condensed in a single point of almost infinite temperature and density. In the first tiny fraction of a second, this exploded outward to increase its volume 10^{100} times. Over the next thirty-four minutes, the first soup of quarks and electrons continued

---

10. Harold J. Morowitz, *The Emergence of Everything: How the World Became Complex* (New York: Oxford University Press, 2004).

to expand and cool until it produced neutrinos, antineutrinos, protons, helium nuclei, and deuterium. By 700,000 years after the Big Bang, the universe was cool enough to produce stable atoms. At that point it was still one thousand times smaller than it is today.

In the story of the divine Heart, the "Big Bang" is the exploding-forth of the vast fountain of divine love from the Heart of God. Because it is infinite, it appears (from our finite perspective) as both tremendously small (the infinitely dense, hot point) and tremendously large (the expanding universe only a fraction of a second later). As the eternal love of God manifests itself in matter, it gives it its content, direction, and form. At this early stage, structures (the first particles and the emerging atoms) are high in energy but low in complexity. The universe is flaming forth, but it is not yet evident what it will become.

2. *The emergence of stars, galaxies, and elements.* If things had been only infinitesimally different, the particle-soup of the early universe could have simply remained as soup, or it could have been drawn back to nothing in a "Big Crunch." Instead, it continued to expand and to form more and more complex structures. Slight variations in density in different parts of the soup formed molecular clouds, which in turn condensed and increased in temperature to become protostars. When these became hot enough, nuclear fusion began to take place in their cores, producing vast amounts of energy as well as new kinds of atomic nuclei. Stars grouped themselves into vast galaxies and went through cycles of changes, finally either decaying or exploding. These processes eventually created the most significant elements of the periodic table, sending them off into space as stardust.

While most scientists are extremely hesitant to ascribe teleology to the vast original chaos of the cosmos, in 1973 physicist Brandon Carter gave a lecture pointing out what he called the "anthropic principle." This is the fact that "From the first nanosecond—against all probability—the cosmos has been so arranged as to make the emergence of life a high probability." The evidence for this is that the discovered values of basic physical constants such as the rate of expansion, the four basic forces (strong and weak nuclear forces, electromagnetism, gravity), and the particle-antiparticle ratio in the early universe are "precisely the values you need if you want to have a universe capable of producing carbon-based life."[11]

While Carter's term "anthropic principle" may go a bit too far in assuming that this evidence necessarily points to the eventual appearance of *Homo sapiens*, it does provide evidence of a universe sent forth with a built-in direction of evolution. Over billions of years love was urgently yet hiddenly at work in the creation of stars, galaxies, and all the elements that are needed for life to flourish, become complex, and manifest more and more of the qualities of the heart. When we say that the stars are our ancestors and that we are made of stardust, we are expressing a literal truth about the universe that has produced us.[12]

3. *The emergence of the solar system and planet Earth.* Many, if not most, of the stars that formed had clouds of stardust circulating around them. Over time, a series of violent collisions led to the aggregation of the circulating matter into larger entities such as asteroids and planets, forming a solar system around some stars. Astronomers have confirmed the existence of

---

11. David Toolan, *At Home in the Cosmos* (Maryknoll, NY: Orbis Books, 2001), 175.

12. Brian Swimme and Mary Evelyn Tucker, *Journey of the Universe* (New Haven: Yale University Press, 2011), 28–29.

thirty-two hundred solar systems in our own Milky Way galaxy, and they extrapolate that there are trillions upon trillions of them in the universe. So far, however, they have not been able to confirm that life exists on any planet other than Earth.

The Earth came into existence four and a half billion years ago as a rock 8000 miles in diameter situated in an orbit 93 million miles from its star, the Sun. The first 200 million years of Earth's existence were extremely violent as volcanic activity and meteoric impacts sorted the rocky materials into layers: core, mantle, asthenosphere, lithosphere, crust, and ocean. The domain that would support life formed on the surface of the planet through additional violent processes that reshaped patterns and cycles among the rocks (lithosphere), water (hydrosphere), and air (atmosphere). All these geospheres were extremely dynamic non-equilibrium systems, continually exchanging materials and energy with each other. The relative planetary equilibrium that James Lovelock described in Gaia Theory did not yet exist, as it depends on the activity and interaction of billions of living creatures.

The conditions for life, however, were being prepared, particularly with the combination of an ideal distance from the sun (not too hot, not too cold), a wide variety of available elements, and an abundance of water. As with the anthropic principle, one can marvel that the Earth came into existence with conditions so perfectly suited for multiple forms of life to thrive. To this date life has not been located anywhere else in the universe, although it would be hard to believe that in such a vast universe populated by trillions of solar systems there would not be any other planets where the conditions also fell together in just the right way. Still, these conditions are hardly to be taken for granted; it seems that they may be extremely rare, even in a vast universe that (we are proposing) was sent forth to incarnate the love of the Heart of God.

4. *The emergence of life.* The earliest forms of life appeared on Earth about a half billion years after the Earth was formed. Much remains undiscovered about how life came to be. Harold Morowitz, who specialized in this field, believed that the emergence of life was preceded by the development of the processes of intermediary metabolism, centered around the Krebs cycle. This is the metabolic center of all life, for out of it comes the synthesis of sugars, fats, amino acids, nucleic acids, vitamins, and cofactors. Over a period of 200 million years or less, beginning most likely in hot sea vents, these metabolic processes somehow produced protocells and then prokaryotic organisms with membranes, cell walls, and ribosomes. Protocells no longer exist, but four billion years later two to four million species of prokaryotes are still flourishing among us.

Although today the tiny size and simplicity of these creatures may not gain much respect from us, Morowitz calls prokaryotes the "universal ancestor."[13] It is a breathtaking moment: at last the livingness of God has begun to manifest in matter, in a creature with motility, self-reproduction, and at least a modicum of intentional behavior (e.g., food-seeking and danger-avoiding). The early prokaryotes gave rise to both the bacteria and the archaea, as well as to the eukaryotes—that is, all the rest of us, whether microbe, fungus, plant, or animal.

Eukaryotes differ from prokaryotes in that their cells have a membrane-bound cell nucleus as well as structures called organelles. As we have noted, Lynn Margulis postulated that these came to be when one prokaryote loosened its cell boundary to engulf another, and the two then lived together in a mutually beneficial symbiotic relationship. It required two billion years, however, before this new, more complex form of organism became established. One of the most important inventions of the

---

13. Morowitz, *The Emergence of Everything*, 83.

eukaryotes was sexual reproduction—which is both "a programmed method of combining genetic information"[14] and an astonishing new structure of mutually beneficial affiliation between individuals. The emergence of eukaryotes, even at the single-cell level, demonstrates an initial foray into manifesting the heart's urges toward relationality and community.

5. *The emergence of multicellular, chordate, and vertebrate life.* For eons, the Heart of God experimented ceaselessly to discover fuller ways to reveal itself in creation. Single-celled organisms formed colonies, then these began to differentiate functions, eventually emerging into multicellular organisms. Of these, three major lines began to emerge: the fungi, the plants, and the animals. To solve the problem of signaling between different parts of the organism, many members of the animal line developed neurons that could transmit electrical signals over distance. They also developed sensory organs and a digestive tract with mouth and anus. Along the branch that would lead to vertebrates, a basic animal body plan emerged: bilateral symmetry with a greater concentration of neurons near the front where eyes and mouth reside, a neuronal cord running from front to rear, and an anus to expel waste at the rear. Thus, for three billion years the heart's qualities of dynamism, self-sustenance, and glimmers of intelligence continually developed.

About 520 million years ago, fish emerged and exploded into many different species, characterized by increasingly complex brains as well as nervous systems, digestive systems, circulatory systems, and respiratory systems. The largest group exhibited the basic vertebrate skeletal plan including the spine and two sets of paired fins. All these organs, systems, and body plans developed as the best available solutions to problems that were posed to living creatures seeking to feed, reproduce, and

---

14. Morowitz, *The Emergence of Everything*, 91.

thrive. It is important to note that for every development noted there were other experiments that resulted in organisms who operated differently, some of whose evolutionary lines continue until today. As we will see in a future chapter, nature is nothing if not profligate in strangeness and diversity!

6. *The emergence of amphibians, reptiles, and dinosaurs.* Up to this point, essentially all multicellular life existed in the oceans. About 500 million years ago plants invaded the land masses, followed another 100 million years later by enterprising fish who sought to feed in this new niche. Over time their swim bladders became proto-lungs to breathe air while their fins modified into legs for motility on land. Most of these early amphibians still laid their eggs in water and had a larval stage that also lived in water. The next set of innovations came yet another 100 million years or so later with the reptiles, whose young are fertilized internally, deposited in eggs with their own food supply, and emerge at a demi-adult stage (rather than as larvae). Many reptiles can live entirely on land. The need for internal fertilization makes sexual dimorphism (male/female) a more prominent feature of these organisms.

The giant reptiles called dinosaurs dominated land ecosystems between 245 and 66 million years ago. In them, as well as in other reptiles, we can see the heart qualities of assertiveness, watchfulness, and territoriality emerging to lay a foundation for meaning-seeking behavior.

7. *The emergence of mammals.* Small mammals first appeared about 178 million years ago. They were different from reptiles in that instead of laying eggs that hatch tiny creatures largely able to care for themselves, mammals gave birth to a smaller number of offspring and invested considerable time and energy in nursing and preparing them for adulthood. This led to larger brains, an enhanced role for affectivity and

relationality, and new varieties of skills. Many mammals continue to live in collaborative kin groups throughout their lives. Here we see the key heart-qualities of affectivity, social skills, and personal loyalty increasingly coming to the fore.

Even during the dinosaur era mammals were quite diverse, but when a cataclysmic event—probably an asteroid strike—led to the extinction of the dinosaurs about 66 million years ago, these creatures took advantage of the sudden availability of many new niches. They were able to increase in size and become the dominant species in most ecosystems. As many as 6,400 mammal species have been identified.

8. *The emergence of proto-humans and Homo sapiens.* Human evolution is complex, and much is not yet known. Genetic evidence shows that humans evolved from arboreal mammals who intensified their grasping skills and reduced their reliance on smell in favor of vision. From them came the primates, who had more refined hands and larger brains that provided them with enhanced behavioral plasticity and more ability to pass on learned information to offspring. These capabilities meant that they could adapt more flexibly to new habitats and changes in circumstances. The line of primates that would produce humans diverged from that which produced the orangutangs about twenty million years ago. At eight million years ago it diverged from the gorilla line, and at seven million years ago from that of the chimpanzees and bonobos.

Hominins (proto-humans) were characterized by bipedalism and an enlarged cerebral cortex. Over seven million years, a series of hominin species came forth that exhibited gradual increases in toolmaking and social skills, thus giving new opportunities for the reflection of the living Heart of God. The first members of our own "Homo" or human genus appeared about 2.3 million years ago and began to demonstrate increasing skill in making and using tools. As early as one million years ago, some of them learned how to control fire for cooking and warmth. At least eight different species of humans existed—often several at the same time—before our own species, *Homo sapiens*, emerged about 300,000 years ago. *Homo sapiens* actually interbred with at least four of these other human species, who bequeathed some of their DNA into our current genetic makeup. For example, persons of European ancestry typically have 2–3 percent Neandertal DNA. Interbreeding with the last other human species, the Denisovans, may have continued until as recently as 15,000 years ago in Papua New Guinea.

Homo sapiens originally evolved in Africa. Around 100,000 years ago, migrations began that eventually led to human populations on every continent. Tool use for hunting and gathering became increasingly sophisticated, which may have been the context in which human language evolved.[15] It was only about 12,000 years ago, however, that humans began to cultivate fields, domesticate animals for food, and live in larger, more elaborate and permanent settlements. Between 5,500 and 3,000 years ago, writing was invented four times in different parts of the world. All that went before this invention we normally call "prehistory," while "history" comprises the relatively short period since that time.

9. *The emergence of Jesus, the Christ.* About two thousand years ago, Jesus was born as a member of the human species in the land of Galilee. As an adult he would be known as the Christ,

---

15. Michael Balter, "Human Language May Have Evolved to Help Our Ancestors Make Tools," *Science*, January 13, 2015, https://www.science.org/content/article/human-language-may-have-evolved-help-our-ancestors-make-tools.

the Anointed One of God, sent to reconcile all things to God. According to the story I am unfolding here, he came forth in the web of life as a human being to complete the manifestation of God's Living Heart on Earth. As David Toolan put it, in Jesus "the cosmos finally finds adequate soul-space, a cavern of interiority big enough to contain the fullness of divine love and compassion."[16] In the historical Jesus, then, a definitive emergence takes place: the created world bears a heart capable of embracing it completely with love. Even though we could say truthfully that God "always" loved the world completely, this is the first time (as far as we know) that this capacity emerges within creation itself.

Describing Jesus as "emergent" raises some tricky theological issues. Christian orthodoxy rejects the idea that the incarnation occurs at the same level of natural phenomena as, say, the appearance of a new animal species. One way to think about it would be to invoke Lynn Margulis's insight into how the loosening of boundaries between symbiotic species can open the possibility for a new type of creature to emerge. In the case of the incarnation, the symbiosis is between the divine and the natural. The divine, of course, cannot be reduced to simply a "part" of the natural world, so "symbiosis" is an analogy rather than, strictly speaking, a description. As Arthur Peacocke put it, God acts by embracing and permeating creation holistically rather than by intervening in one of its parts. The incarnation is evolutionary and emergent in the sense that creation had to arrive at a point of readiness for it to manifest in this way, but theologically it is still a free act of divine grace that is not constrained by natural processes. The incarnation is a "loosening of boundaries" between God and creation, allowing one who is both human and divine to come forth.

---

16. Toolan, *At Home in the Cosmos*, 206.

Since Jesus was a human being, it is tempting to think that he came only for the sake of the species into which he was born. Following this line of thought, one could presume that the human species is the only one of concern to God, and that other species are only here as resources or backdrop for human flourishing. A more accurate point of view, however, would be that just as he was born in one small nation but had a mission to all nations, so he was born in one species but had a mission of reconciliation for all. God's Heart is most fully manifested in the entire web of diverse creatures rather than in any single type of creature—even human beings. The next chapter explores the implications of this.

FOR REFLECTION AND PRACTICE:

Lie on your back outside at night and ponder the vastness of the universe. Let your heart expand into this vastness. Who are you in the midst of all this?

On another occasion, lie face downwards on the ground and examine the tiny intricacies of soil, plant, fungi, and plant life that you discover there. Where is God in this for you?

FOR FURTHER READING:

Mary Evelyn Tucker and Brian Swimme, *The Journey of the Universe* (New Haven, CT: Yale University Press, 2011).

Ilia Delio, *The Unbearable Wholeness of Being: God, Evolution, and the Power of Love* (Maryknoll, NY: Orbis, 2013).

John Haught, *The New Cosmic Story: Inside Our Awakening Universe* (New Haven, CT: Yale University Press, 2020).

5

A WILD AND QUEER KINDOM

If there is a Heart at the heart of the world, what kind of world does it engender? Sometimes in our fantasies we imagine that an infinitely loving God would create a world that is something like a well-ordered nursery, beautifully appointed with everything the children need, sparkling clean, and carefully watched over night and day by benevolent caretakers. But the actual world engendered by Heart is not like that at all. Its primary characteristic is that it is supremely "wild."

Love of the wild

Dictionaries tend to define "wild" negatively, as "not tame" and "out of control." The wild, from the point of view of many of those who think they do not live there, is a chaotic and violent place to be avoided and/or brought under control. The truth, however, is that we come from the wild; ultimately, it is our home. The fecundity, vastness, and mystery of the wild may frighten us, but it also attracts and heals us. California "mountain man" John Muir spoke for many when he looked at the chaos of wildness and saw holy wonder where others see danger. He wrote: "Storms of every sort, torrents, earth-quakes, cataclysms, convulsions of nature, etc., however mysterious and lawless at first sight they may seem, are only harmonious notes in the song of creation, varied expressions of God's love."[1]

A positive definition of wildness comes from Zen practitioner and poet Gary Snyder. He wrote that wild animals are "free agents, each with its own endowments living within natural systems," while wild land is "a place where the original and potential vegetation and fauna are intact and in full interaction and the landforms are entirely the result of nonhuman forces."[2] In this perspective, to be "wild" is to be fully alive, operating without hindrance according to one's innate capabilities, creatively constructing relationships of mutually beneficial exchange with all the beings one encounters. This is the kind of world that Heart creates.

If we define wilderness as a place where the flora and fauna can live and interact totally according to their own predilections without any influence of humans, it is arguable that at this point in history there is no wilderness left on Earth. Wildness, however, is another matter. We will find wildness wherever we look for it, whether in the concrete deserts of the cities or in the strange depths of our own psyches. Tom Brown tells the story of asking the Apache grandfather of his best friend Rick to tell the boys about his adventures in the wilderness. The old man captivated them for hours with tales about a jungle-like place with huge trees, boulders of pure quartz, and all manner of bizarre creatures stalking and playing with one

1. John Muir, *John Muir: Spiritual Writings*, ed. Tim Flinders, Modern Spiritual Masters Series (Maryknoll, NY: Orbis Books, 2013).

2. Gary Snyder, *The Practice of the Wild: Essays* (San Francisco: North Point Press, 1990), 9–10.

another. Then they asked him where this place was. "Rick's front lawn," he answered.

Chastened, the boys went and lay down on the grass in the front yard. Brown writes:

> Within moments I was hopelessly lost in this jungle of grass. ... There was a whole world down there that I would not have believed could be so beautiful or intriguing. Tiny plants and fungi littered the grass forest floor. Miniature stones took on odd shapes, colors, and textures; some were dark brown, others black, some even crystal clear. The very earth itself was a marvelous blend of tiny jewel-like boulders, minuscule tracks, bits of plants, and sundry other mysterious items. The earth was littered with bits and pieces of the animal world: insect parts, hair, claws, whiskers, tiny teeth, bits of skulls. There were seeds of all descriptions, flower parts—so many other things that a list could easily fill a notebook.[3]

A manicured front lawn does not look like a wilderness, but at ground level wildness reigns. Wildness is the ineradicable base state of the Earth and everything on it. It is our base state, as well. The poet Rainer Maria Rilke put it this way:

> ... But when I lean over the chasm of myself—
> it seems my God is dark
> and like a web: a hundred roots
> silently drinking.
> This is the ferment I grow out of ...[4]

3. Tom Brown, *Tom Brown's Field Guide to the Forgotten Wilderness* (New York: Berkley Books, 1987), 5.

4. Rainer Maria Rilke, *Rilke's Book of Hours: Love Poems to God*, trans. Anita Barrows and Joanna Macy (New York: Riverhead Books, 2005), 49.

Our challenge, especially now, is to make friends with the ferment and wildness of ourselves, our world, and our God. This is not easy because, as Brown goes on to say, the wild is also the arena of life-and-death struggles. In the grass jungle he observed the drama of spider predation, aphid parasitism, and fungal disease unfolding in the midst of the exuberance of beauty and diversity. Our wildness is why we often struggle with our disruptive emotions and moods, and it is also why an undertone of contentiousness frequently tinges even our best relationships. Yet repressing and running away from the jungle in our psyche is the least effective strategy for finding relative peace with ourselves, others, and our world. It is only in welcoming wildness that we will ultimately find the seedbed of the kindom of God.

Peace amid the tempest

The most famous biblical passage that addresses this is Isaiah 11:6–9, which has become known as the "peaceable kingdom" passage. It portrays the coming of the Davidic Messiah as ending all enmity and predation, even among wild animals:

> The wolf lives with the lamb,
> The panther lies down with the kid.
> Calf and lion cub feed together
> With a little boy to lead them.
> The cow and the bear make friends,
> Their young lie down together.
> The lion eats straw like the ox.
> The infant plays over the cobra's hole;
> Into the viper's lair
> The young child puts his hand.
> They do no hurt, no harm
> On all my holy mountain

For the country is filled with the knowledge of Yahweh
As the waters swell the sea.

This is a beautiful and inspiring vision. Yet it may not be the most helpful biblical text for assisting us in making friends with our wildness and recognizing our kinship with wild creatures. The lion who eats straw instead of meat, or even the wolf who will lie down with a lamb, are not creatures we are ever likely to meet in the wild. A more apropos perspective comes from Job 38–40, where Yahweh, speaking out of a wild tempest, offers an astonishing exposition of real wild creatures and our relationship with them.

In the first two chapters of the book, Job's wealth and virtue are extolled—and then he loses his possessions, his health, and his reputation. The next thirty-six chapters are occupied with endless speeches and arguments among Job and his friends as they try to make sense of what to them is a scandal; virtuous persons, according to their philosophy, should flourish. But the first line of chapter 38 essentially demolishes all the verbiage that went before, as Yahweh shouts from the heart of the tempest: "Who is this obscuring my designs with his empty-headed words?"

I highly recommend reading these chapters, which are too rich even to attempt to summarize! Instead of answering Job or attending to his needs, Yahweh blasts him with an extended celebration of the wildness and grandeur of the Earth and its creatures—including their strangeness and violence. In this exuberant testimony, humans do not even appear; it is wild beasts that God repeatedly admires and professes care for. Yahweh lets Job know in no uncertain terms that this vast, terrifying, unimaginably diverse cosmos was not created to serve Job, but rather that Job is going to have to find his tiny, humble place within the wild multiplicity of what God has created. These wild and free animals for whom God cares will clearly never be dominated by humans; they prance about and laugh at puny human efforts to control or understand them. As one author puts it, even God does not claim to understand them![5]

Finally, Job is silenced; he concludes, "I knew you [before] only by hearsay; but now, having seen you with my own eyes, I retract all I have said, and in dust and ashes, I repent" (Job 42:5–6). Biblical scholar Barry Huff sums up by affirming that this theophany "moves Job from isolation to interconnected-ness, from self-absorption to cosmic awe, and from perceiving God as his personal persecutor to witnessing the Creator's ex-pansive embrace."[6] Job has begun to accept his own wildness— which includes his vulnerability to suffering—and his kinship as one (but only one) of the wild creatures of God.

Jesus in the wilderness

An enigmatic text from the Gospel of Mark can add to our in-sight into God's relationship with the wild world. Mark 1:12–13 reads, "Immediately after [Jesus's baptism] the Spirit drove him out into the wilderness, and he remained there for forty days, and was tempted by Satan. He was with the wild beasts, and the angels looked after him." The text clearly makes a par-allel between Jesus's time of testing in the wilderness and the Exodus, when the Israelites were tested for forty days in the wilderness before being able to enter the promised land. The line, "He was with the wild beasts," however, has engendered much discussion. Some scholars assert that danger and violence

---

are the qualities most often associated with "the wild" in the Bible.[7] This view emphasizes the hostility and dangerousness of the wild beasts, aligning them with Satan as an element of the "testing" that Jesus must undergo in the wilderness.

Yet the wilderness is also seen in the Bible as a special place of intimate encounter with God. Another group of scholars, then, takes the opposite tack and sees Jesus being "with" the wild beasts as an indication that he is living with them intimately and companionably. Richard Bauckham, for example, connects this to the "peaceable kingdom" text of Isaiah 11:1–6 and sees it as an affirmation of Jesus as the Davidic Messiah who returns the world to its original Edenic state.[8] Another scholar, Charles Gieschen, finds an even better precursor in Isaiah 43:19–20, where Yahweh says: "I am making a road in the wilderness, paths in the wilds; the wild beasts will honor me...." Gieschen notes that Mark had just quoted Isaiah 40:3 in verses 2 and 3, and that the text of Isaiah 43 picks up again on the language of the "way in the wilderness." In this view, Mark is presenting Jesus as Yahweh himself, whom the animals honor because he cares for them.[9]

A related foundational text in the Hebrew Bible is Genesis 9:9–10, which reports that the very first covenant that Yahweh made with human beings was also made with all living creatures. After the flood, Yahweh says to Noah: "See, I am now establishing my covenant with you and your descendants after

---

7. J. P. Heil, "Jesus with the Wild Animals in Mark 1:13," *Catholic Biblical Quarterly* 68, no. 1 (2006): 63–78.

8. Richard Bauckham, "Jesus and the Wild Animals (Mark 1:13): A Christological Image for the Ecological Age," in *Jesus of Nazareth: Lord and Christ*, ed. Joel B. Green and Max Turner (Grand Rapids, MI: Eerdmans, 1994), 3–21.

9. C. A. Gieschen, "Why Was Jesus with the Wild Beasts (Mark 1:13)?," *Concordia Theological Quarterly* 73, no. 1 (2009): 77–80.

you and with every living creature that was with you: the birds, the tame animals, and all the wild animals that were with you." God's care and kindom are for all living beings, not humans alone. Bauckham summarizes his consideration of Mark's text with a similar view:

> Mark's image of Jesus' companionable presence with the wild animals affirms their independent value for themselves and for God. He does not adopt them into the human world, but lets them be themselves in peace, leaving them in their wilderness, affirming them as creatures who share the world with us in the community of God's creation.[10]

In short, the fact that wild creatures, from viruses to rats to sharks, may at times be inconvenient or even life-threatening for human beings does not detract from their being equally members of the kindom that God has created and longs to accompany into the fullness of life. Pope Francis affirmed as much in his 2015 encyclical *Laudato Si'* when he wrote that "The ultimate purpose of other creatures is not to be found in us," but rather, "Every creature is...the object of the Father's tenderness, who gives it its place in the world. Even the fleeting life of the least of beings is the object of his love, and in its few seconds of existence, God enfolds it with his affection."[11] Such a profound shift away from anthropocentrism is at first a shock for most of us, yet accepting it opens a door to a way of living among the community of creatures in a humble, tender, wonder-filled, and companionable way—as Jesus did.

---

10. Bauckham, "Jesus and the Wild Animals," 20.

11. Pope Francis, *On Care for Our Common Home: Laudato Si'* (Washington, DC: United States Conference of Catholic Bishops, 2015), paras. 83, 77.

Chaos and exuberance

Way back in 1927, the English biologist J. B. S. Haldane wrote that "the universe is not only queerer than we suppose, but queerer than we can suppose."[12] In his context, the word "queer" meant odd, peculiar, eccentric, or "off" in some way. While (as we will see below) the word "queer" has taken on different connotations since then, Haldane presumably meant something like what Annie Dillard meant when she wrote, "The whole creation is one lunatic fringe.... No claims of any and all revelations could be so far-fetched as a single giraffe."[13] Like Job being bowled over when Yahweh roars from the heart of the tempest, Haldane's and Dillard's minds are blown when they look closely at any single thing that has come forth from the wondrous chaos of creation. A giraffe, the tangled jungle hiding in the front lawn, the mysteries of a quark or of a trillion galaxies, the poignant inscrutability of what lurks in a human heart—wherever we look, we find both astonishing beauty and unaccountable strangeness. The wild world, inner and outer, is indeed "queerer than we can suppose."

In recent decades the science of what is called "chaos theory" has profoundly revised the concepts of scientific laws, norms, and predictability. Chaos theory studies events to which a very large number of random (that is, chaotic) fluctuations contribute. An example would be quadrillions of molecules in the air bumping against one another as well as encountering various land features and temperature variations. It turns out that over time the chaos will self-organize into patterns (in this

---

12. J. B. S. Haldane, *Possible Worlds and Other Papers* (New York: Harper and Brothers, 1928), 298–99.

13. Annie Dillard, *Pilgrim at Tinker Creek* (New York: Harper Perennial Modern Classics, 2013), 146.

case, of wind movement), but the exact course and form of these patterns cannot be predicted. Moreover, what transpires in such self-organization processes will sometimes be totally outside the bounds of what is considered "typical." As Sally Goerner put it, "Time and again, nonlinear models show that apparently aberrant, illogical behavior is, in fact, a completely lawful part of the system."[14] What seems "strange" or "off" to us may simply be the unexpected creativity of the wild world.

While chaos theory was originally developed in relation to large-scale physical phenomena, it has more recently been applied to social and biological phenomena as well. The more traditional view of evolution assumes that every variation in a species' coloration, morphological structure, behavior, and so forth is passed on only if it gives that individual creature a direct reproductive advantage. A chaos theory perspective suggests that multiple variations occur and may even flourish within the wild chaos of nature simply because of the fecund creativity of the vast number of interconnecting factors. Goerner explains: "A single system may exhibit many different forms of behavior —all the result of the same basic dynamic. One equation, many faces. A corollary to this idea is that a system may have ... multiple competing forms of behavior, each perhaps a hairsbreadth away, each representing stable mutual-effect organization."[15] There is rarely only one way to solve an evolutionary challenge; chaotic creativity may throw forth many ways, some of them startlingly strange, and all "successful."

Chaos theory, then, is a scientific way of accounting for the astonishing diversity and strangeness we encounter any time we look closely at the natural world. Take bird adornment, as

---

14. Sally Goerner, "Chaos, Evolution, and Deep Ecology," in *Chaos Theory in Psychology and the Life Sciences*, ed. Robin Robertson and Allan Combs (Mahwah, NJ: Lawrence Erlbaum Associates, 1995), 17–38.

15. Goerner, "Chaos, Evolution, and Deep Ecology," 24.

just one example: the scissortail's sweeping tail, the peacock's many-hued fantail, the bowerbird's dance, the hornbill's beak, the hummingbird's translucent shimmer—who could dream these things up? Rather than reducing all this simply to functional explanations, Bruce Bagemihl proposes instead a principle of "biological exuberance." He writes, "The essence of Biological Exuberance is that natural systems are driven as much by abundance and excess as they are by limitation and practicality."[16] The wild experiments of nature look more like the contents of an art school attic than like the lean, mean, strictly efficient structures of a capitalistic business!

The queer kindom

As we learn more about the ways of the wild, Haldane's comment about the queerness of the universe is turning out to have been prophetic in ways he presumably never intended. Even in his time, a secondary meaning of "queer" was as a pejorative slur applied to homosexual people. Since then, the meaning of the word has evolved. Beginning in the 1980s, LGBT people began to claim the title "queer" positively to celebrate the diverse forms of non-heteronormative sexuality. While the original meaning of "strangeness" is still extant, the primary meaning of "queer" today is a broad reference to any form of sexual or gender expression that "colors outside the lines" of cultural norms regarding male masculinity, female femininity, and how they are supposed to relate to one another. However, "queer" can also be used even more broadly to point toward a way of seeing that rejects all culturally imposed binaries such as male/female, gay/straight, nature/nurture, and us/them.

---

16. Bruce Bagemihl, *Biological Exuberance: Animal Homosexuality and Natural Diversity*, Stonewall Inn Editions (New York: St. Martin's Press, 2000), 215.

Bagemihl's book *Biological Exuberance: Animal Homosexuality and Natural Diversity* dispels any doubt that the wild world is "queerer than we suppose"—in the new meaning as well as the old. The print version of the book is 751 pages, and it is not recommended for light reading since it consists of a rather mind-numbing review of all the scientific literature up to the time of publication (2000) on homosexuality and transgender in animals, birds, and some fish. Same-sex behavior reviewed includes copulation, other forms of sexual stimulation, pair bonding, and co-parenting as well as transgender (e.g., creatures of one biological sex that look or behave in ways considered typical of the other sex).

It turns out that research up to that point had found one or more of these same-sex behaviors in 450 different animal species. Bagemihl notes that a great many species have never been studied on this question, especially because until relatively recently homosexuality in animals was regarded as a rare and cringe-worthy aberration that respectable scientists either ignored or explained away. Moreover, in many species sexual activity is not easily observed and/or the sexes are not easily distinguished, making accurate research quite challenging. Bagemihl gives the rather humorous example of a set of King Penguins whose sexual activity was observed for seven years with the initial guiding assumption that all the pairings were heterosexual. The researchers soon became confused as some observed sexual behavior did not seem to conform to their heteronormative expectations. At the end of their seven-year observation period, the researchers finally discovered that the sex of all but one of the birds had been wrongly identified, so that all their assumptions about which pairings were heterosexual and which were homosexual were mistaken![17] Thus, it is likely that even the massive amount of literature reviewed in

---

17. Bagemihl, *Biological Exuberance*, 94–96.

Bagemihl's book reveals only the tip of the iceberg on the topic of "queerness" in the natural world.

In the 450 species studied, all sorts of patterns of same-sex behavior prevail, making it impossible to make big generalizations other than that the natural behavior of animals is vastly more queer than most have ever imagined. In some species, all or many individuals are bisexual, copulating with both sexes freely or spending some parts of their lives in sexual activity within same-sex groups and other periods of time in heterosexual mating relationships. In other species a certain percentage of individuals (anywhere from 1 percent to 20 percent or more) appear to be exclusively homosexual, choosing same-sex liaisons even when members of the opposite sex seek their company. Same-sex pair bonding is found in a significant number of species, among them grizzlies (usually female pairs) and mallard ducks (usually male pairs). These bonded relationships may or may not include sexual activity. They also may or may not include parenting, with offspring obtained either by brief heterosexual matings or by adoption. In general, animal same-sex pairs who raise young have equal or better success compared to opposite-sex pairs.

Transgender is also quite common, with many species including individuals who are genetically one sex but cross gender lines in their appearance and/or their behavior, as well as (sometimes) in their sexual inclinations. In some species, such as ruffed grouse, this is "institutionalized," as there are four kinds of males, each looking different and tending toward different heterosexual, same-sex, and/or asexual behaviors. In addition to all this, some species include celibate individuals who live their whole lives without engaging in sexual activity with either sex. These individuals are often among the healthiest members of their species, since mating and reproducing are draining and, sometimes, dangerous activities.

Bonobos (a type of chimp), who are one of humanity's closest relatives, are famous as a species in which virtually every individual participates enthusiastically in both same-sex and opposite-sex activity, with as many as 40 to 50 percent of all sexual encounters being with partners of the same sex. For common chimpanzees (a different species) the ratio of same-sex to heterosexual activity is closer to about 4 percent for adults and 15 percent for adolescents, thus demonstrating that even closely related species may have quite different patterns of same-sex sexuality. When it comes to specifics, we cannot generalize from any species to any other, nor from animals to humans (or vice versa). What we can say, however, is that in the natural world the simplistic binary assumed by heteronormativity—that is, that any sexual activity that is not between a male behaving in a masculine manner and a female behaving in a feminine manner is pathological—emphatically does not hold up. The exuberant abundance of the wild, queer world has brought forth and sustained just about every pattern of sexuality that one can imagine.

A non-binary God

The fact that the created world does not adhere to the heteronormative sexual binary is less surprising when one takes into account that the Creator is non-binary. While even applying the term "non-binary" to God is a projection from the human experience of sexuality, it is far better than identifying God with only one half of the male-female binary. Not so many years ago, it was a hard sell to convince undergraduates that God is not male. Trying to explain that feminine pronouns are just as appropriate as masculine ones when talking about God, I would look out over the room and see perplexity and doubt on most of the faces. While a few (usually young women) might be intrigued by the idea that God could be imaged as female, even they could rarely embrace the idea that ultimately God is neither male nor female.

A large part of the problem, of course, was that the biblical tradition, which continues to shape not only church language but that of broader Western culture as well, does envision God almost exclusively as male. The minority of biblical texts where God is imaged as female were rarely known or noticed by anyone other than feminist scholars who went in search of them. But the other part of the problem for the undergrads in those days was that they could not imagine a person who was not either male or female. Some of them were able to articulate the deep uneasiness they felt: for them, a person who did not fit into the gender binary would not be a person, but some kind of amorphous or even monstrous "it."

Times have changed! I haven't been teaching undergraduates for quite a few years now, but I've heard from those who do that the reaction now is quite different. A professor teaching this theme may still get some significant resistance from biblical literalists—in fact, maybe even more than I did thirty years ago. These students are convinced that biblical evidence proves that God has revealed that he is male. A significant portion of the class, however, is likely to "get" quite easily the idea that God is non-binary. The concept is familiar to them, and they actually know people who identify themselves in that way. Their imaginations have been set free from the gender binary to recognize that sexuality comes in all sorts of patterns and styles. They also know from personal experience that non-binary and other queer people are at least as interesting, relatable, and "normal" as anyone else. They quickly grasp the logic that God cannot be identified with only one kind of human being, but must include all.

Jesus and sexuality

But what about Jesus, who as far as we know was identified as male throughout his historical life? Elizabeth A. Johnson explains that while having a sex is a constituent dimension of Jesus's human nature, that is not the case for divine nature. The problem, she notes, is that "the androcentric imagination occasions a certain leakage of Jesus's human maleness into the divine nature, so that maleness appears to be of the essence of the God made known in Christ."[18] In other words, if we adhere to the Chalcedonian injunction that Jesus has both human and divine natures without their being mixed together or confused, we will understand that his human maleness cannot be projected as divine maleness.

Clarifying that God is non-binary does not conclude debate about the sex and sexuality of Jesus. If sexuality is a constitutive dimension of being human, and Jesus comes among us as the premier divinely-anointed model of humanity, we cannot avoid this question simply by saying that the gospels present him as a male human being and say nothing explicit about his sexual feelings or interests. Questions have been raised about his sexual identity, his sexual orientation, and even his biological sex.

Taking the last question first, Susannah Cornwall notes that the fact that there is no evidence that Jesus's biological maleness was ever questioned by those around him does not preclude the possibility that he was actually intersex.[19] An in-

---

18. Elizabeth A. Johnson, *She Who Is: The Mystery of God in Feminist Theological Discourse* (New York: Crossroad, 1992), 152.

19. Susannah Cornwall, "Sex Otherwise: Intersex, Christology, and the Maleness of Jesus," *Journal of Feminist Studies in Religion* 30, no. 2 (2014): 23–39, https://doi.org/10.2979/jfemistudreli.30.2.23.

tersex person has biological features of both sexes. In some intersex conditions, the person's outward physical presentation is that of a conventional male or female while their chromosomal makeup and/or internal organs are completely or partially those of the opposite sex. Even today, with so much more genetic and medical knowledge available, some people may live their entire lives without ever knowing that they have this type of intersex physiology. Cornwall is not arguing that Jesus necessarily *was* intersex, but rather that he *could have been,* despite always being perceived publicly as male. Moreover, two thousand years later there is absolutely no way of verifying one way or the other. The implication is that arguments cannot be built on the presumption that he was male.

As a human being, Jesus not only had a sex (whether male or intersex) but also had a sexual life—that is, he felt erotic longings. Exploring questions about Jesus's sexual identity, sexual orientation, and sexual practice has been quite controversial, as the general preference tends to be to think of him as effortlessly transcending or sublimating all erotic feelings into pure love of God. Embodied erotic attractions, however, may be lived out in many other ways besides genital sex. Carter Heyward, for example, proposes that God's relationship with all creatures is best described as "erotic friendship."[20] For her, all our significant relationships are erotic, in the sense that they involve profound, intimate attractions and longings. These do not have to be oriented toward sexual intercourse for them to be means by which we are created and liberated for the fullness of life. In this perspective, Jesus's erotic relations of tenderness and mutual care with both women and men can be framed as deep, liberating friendships.

---

20. Carter Heyward, *Touching Our Strength: The Erotic as Power and the Love of God* (San Francisco: Harper & Row, 1989).

Nonetheless, one can find arguments put forth that Jesus was married, bisexual, or gay. All such arguments, however, extrapolate beyond the known evidence, since the agenda of the gospel writers did not include explicating Jesus's sexual attractions. One element that often is not sufficiently clarified is that sexuality in the first-century Middle East was not configured in the same way that it is in the twenty-first century West. Male dominance over females was assumed, and marriage and other heterosexual relationships were thought of more in terms of the man's possession of the woman than as mutual loving relations. While an outwardly homosexual lifestyle was regarded as morally contemptible, casual sexual activity between males may have been widely tolerated. As Theodore Jennings puts it, "It seems to have been widely assumed that all men would be attracted to both male and female partners and that at least many, even most, would act upon that attraction."[21]

Jennings suggests that in these circumstances, the gospel writers may have found it easier to depict genuinely mutual, affectionate, and non-dominating relationships occurring between males than between a man and a woman.[22] This may be a helpful way of looking at the very intimate relationship that John portrays between Jesus and the "beloved disciple" who engaged in the unusual behavior of leaning on his chest at the last supper (John 13:21–26). Rather than meaning that Jesus was "gay" as that is understood today, it is a portrayal of what an intimate friendship with Jesus can be like for a disciple, male or female.

Equally significant is how the gospels show Jesus consistently breaking with cultural norms in his relations with women. Perhaps the most often cited example is his dialogue

---

21. Theodore W. Jennings, "The 'Gay' Jesus," in *The Blackwell Companion to Jesus*, ed. Delbert Burkett (Oxford, UK: Wiley-Blackwell, 2010), 451, https://doi.org/10.1002/9781444327946.ch27.

22. Jennings, "The 'Gay' Jesus," 449.

with the Samaritan woman at the well (John 4:4–30). His disciples react with shock when they come back and find that he has been chatting with a woman for some time; no properly socialized adult male Jew would do that! Other examples include his letting a woman with a bad reputation anoint his feet (Luke 7:36–50), and his merciful interaction with the woman caught in adultery (John 8:1–11). Both because they were female and because they were regarded as sinners, all these women should have been firmly disdained by a virtuous male of that culture. Yet Jesus interacted respectfully with them and sought to meet their most authentic needs.

Like his biological sex, the historical Jesus's actual sexual feelings, orientation, identity, and practices cannot be verified. The only evidence we have are the gospels, written many decades later and with different questions in mind than the ones many people today would like answered. However, insofar as they show Jesus repeatedly refusing to take up the roles and behaviors expected of a male in his patriarchically constructed society, we can identify him as living elements of a "non-binary" gender identity. Non-binary persons either refuse both male and female identities, or practice a fluidity between them. This is not to suggest that Jesus consciously practiced the kind of gender fluidity that some non-binary people do today. The gospels depict him not as rejecting his presumed maleness *in toto*, but rather as being entirely unconstrained by the cultural assumptions that went along with it.

Halvor Moxnes notes that when Jesus praises eunuchs in Matthew 19:12, he is lifting up those who had "lost the very sign of their masculinity, their sexual virility, and therefore could not fill the masculine role within the heterosexual system of family, property, and descent."[23] A likely scenario, Moxnes

---

23. Halvor Moxnes, "Jesus in Gender Trouble," *Cross Currents* (New Rochelle, NY) 54, no. 3 (2004): 39.

suggests, is that Jesus and his disciples had been disparagingly called eunuchs, not because they were actually castrated but because they would not take up the expected male "place" of domination and control. They were non-binary in the sense that they responded to other persons, male or female, with individualized respect rather than according to heteronormative expectations. Indeed, M. Shawn Copeland proposes that Jesus is "queer" in the sense that he heartfully embraces and valorizes all bodies, no matter where they stand in regard to what is customarily regarded as normative.[24] Rather than making a claim about his sexual orientation, she is pointing to his binary-rejecting heart.

Radical love and "making kin"

We began this chapter by asking what sort of world is engendered by divine Heart. It turns out to be a world that is wildly and exuberantly diverse—and a world that is "queerer than we can suppose." Patrick S. Cheng writes about how theology is changed when it takes up a queer position—that is, when it questions all binaries and boundaries. He writes that such theology discovers God as "radical love." He continues: "Radical love, I contend, is a love so extreme that it dissolves our existing boundaries, whether they are boundaries that separate us from other people, that separate us from preconceived notions of sexuality and gender identity, or that separate us from God."[25] To his list we might also add the boundaries that separate us from other species and from the interconnected web of life on Earth. It is God whose radical love first breaks down

24. M. Shawn Copeland, *Enfleshing Freedom: Body, Race, and Being, Innovations* (Minneapolis: Fortress Press, 2010), 70–80.

25. Patrick S. Cheng, *Radical Love: An Introduction to Queer Theology* (New York: Seabury Books, 2011), 14.

boundaries—of time and eternity, human and divine, created and uncreated, death and life—and continually pours itself out into a wild and boundless diversity of loved and loving creatures.

Perhaps at this point a note of caution must be introduced. Humanly speaking, even deep love needs boundaries. An infinite God may be capable of complete boundarylessness, but we finite and mortal creatures rarely are. As for reveling in the creativity of chaos and the delight of the wild, this must be tempered by the prudent awareness that there are real dangers out there for our fragile bodies and vulnerable psyches. One of the chief characteristics of wild animals is their vigilance and their hair-trigger readiness to flee, freeze, or fight when danger appears. We too must keep our wild instincts tuned to be ready to protect ourselves and those for whom we care.

But even more important, in this dawning Ecozoic era, is learning how to "make kin." This is Donna Haraway's phrase for the hard work of building relationships of belonging-together with those whom we might find it far easier to keep at a distance. This includes suffering, oppressed, and "strange" humans as well as all the other creatures with whom we share our ecosystems. In an interview Haraway observed, "By kin I mean those who have an enduring, obligatory, non-optional, you-can't-just-cast-that-away-when-it-gets-inconvenient, enduring relatedness that carries consequences."[26] In building kin relationships across boundaries, we engage both obligations and pleasures that are found in no other way.

This is the meaning of kin that makes sense of the "kin-dom" of God. These kin may be of a different culture or species than us, but we still recognize them as family in some way—

---

26. Steve Paulson, "Making Kin: An Interview with Donna Haraway," *LA Review of Books*, December 6, 2019, https://lareviewofbooks.org/article/making-kin-an-interview-with-donna-haraway/.

and we accept the accountability that demands of us. The family of the kindom of God is wild, queer, often overwhelming, and maybe even dangerous at times. But this is where radical love lives.

FOR REFLECTION AND PRACTICE:

Take a long, slow walk around your neighborhood or in a park. Take time to look closely at the creatures you encounter. What do you see that is strange? Beautiful? Surprising? Endearing? Consider how you can "make kin" with some of these creatures.

"Queer" can be defined as rejecting the concept that the world is structured by binaries such as male/female, good/bad, and gay/straight. What do you find personally enlivening or empowering in this idea? Does it correspond with any of your own experience?

FOR FURTHER READING:

David Abram, *Becoming Animal: An Earthly Cosmology* (New York: Vintage, 2010).

Gavin van Horn, Robin Wall Kimmerer, and John Hausdoerffer, eds., *Kinship: Belonging in a World of Relations* (Center for Humans and Nature, 2021).

Gerald G. May, *The Wisdom of Wilderness: Experiencing the Healing Power of Nature* (New York: HarperOne, 2006).

Daniel T. Spencer, *Gay and Gaia: Ethics, Ecology, and the Erotic* (Cleveland: Pilgrim, 1996).

6

CHRIST OF THE FOREST

B efore I moved into the city where I now reside, I lived for a
year in a house where, after only a ten-minute walk, I could
wander freely on semi-wild and relatively unpopulated forest
paths. In that milieu, it was easy to drop into a contemplative
space of delight in the sights, smells, and wildlife encounters of
the forest. In the city, however, the nearby green spaces are
highly tamed and nearly always full of people running, biking,
walking dogs, or chatting with friends. With the exception of
an occasional small child, it is rare to see any of the humans
paying much attention to the green space or wildlife around
them. I couldn't help but feel a bit rattled and distracted when-
ever I went for a walk on those paths. My impression of these
parks was that they had little to offer to my nature-loving soul.

A year or so after moving, I participated in a workshop in
which we were invited to let an animal appear and be our guide
on an imaginative journey. The animal that appeared for me
was a ring-tailed lemur, hanging upside down and watching
me curiously with its big, wide-open eyes. Although it didn't
really take me on a journey, I felt like I was being instructed by
how it moved so slowly, completely at one with the surround-

ing trees and earth and sky, and by its big-eyed curiosity about everything with which it crossed paths. (It has been pointed out that in real life, ring-tailed lemurs do not move slowly; but my imaginary lemur did!)

The next time I went for a walk on the busy park pathways, I went with lemur as my imaginary companion. Slow, big-eyed, at one with the earth, we strolled along in our own world, frequently cooled by the breeze of those passing hurriedly by. It was astonishing to awaken to the utter beauty of that landscape that previously had seemed so uninteresting. Every leaf, flower, seed pod, grass stem, tree trunk, and bird was a new revelation of wonder. As the light wind made intricate dance patterns on the shimmering pond, a thousand subtle variations of color unfolded in sky and water and greenery. Everything sparkled like a bejeweled work of art. The world itself seemed almost divine.

Such experiences are sometimes called "nature mysticism," and many people have experienced similar moments of being bowled over by a holy light that glints within a sunset, or a mountain, or the eyes of a wild animal. These moments often come upon people spontaneously, but they can also be cultivated by practices such as my imaginary "walk with lemur." Christians have often been a bit suspicious of such experiences, for fear they will lead into pantheism—that is, an outright claim that nature is divine. In this chapter, we explore how the reclaiming of such experiences may be a key to a refreshed Christianity for an ecospiritual age.

Jesus in the forests of Paneas

In the winter before his death, Jesus invited his disciples to join him on a journey north to the region of Caesarea Philippi. This was a lush, forested region at the foot of Mount Hermon, just north of what today is called the Golan Heights. Its central feature was a spring gushing from a cave set in a tall, dramatic rock formation. Originally dedicated to a Semitic Ba'al, this spot had from ancient times been claimed as a place of worship and pilgrimage. After Alexander the Great conquered the region in the fourth century BCE, the focus of worship turned to the Greek god Pan and the nearby village became known as Paneas. Pan was the god of the wild, of forests and groves, and of fertility. A jumble of statues, courtyards, and shrines to this popular god grew up on the terrace beneath the cave. In about 20 BCE, however, Herod the Great erected a Roman temple to the deified emperor Caesar Augustus there. Seventeen years later, his son Philip Herod expanded the imperial temple and built a resort city nearby, changing the name of the region to Caesarea Philippi.

When I had the opportunity to join a Holy Land tour in 2017, the group's visit to what is now called the Banias Nature Reserve was one of the most significant moments for me. Although an earthquake in the nineteenth century had collapsed the roof of the cave and reduced the gushing spring to a trickle, the cliff face and the remnants of the pagan shrines were still impressive, as were the nearby forests, trails, and waterfall. Prior to that time, I had imagined Jesus in villages, cities, farmlands, and deserts, but it had never occurred to me that he spent time in forests. I was captivated by the thought of Jesus and his disciples coming on a kind of vacation to this beautiful wooded area, meandering along its quiet paths and marveling at the cascading waterfall. This was a very different image of Jesus, and one that resonated with my own predilection for wild forests and rushing streams.

As is the case with many of the details of Jesus's life, we don't actually know a great deal about what he and his disciples did on their visit to the region of Caesarea Philippi. We know that their weariness by this time must have been bone-deep, especially after the shock of the death of John the Baptist and the dawning realization that a similar fate could be in store for them. It seems likely that after arriving in this well-known vacation area they would have taken time to relax and let the sights, sounds, and smells of the natural world wash over them and refresh their spirits. We can imagine that the impressive rock formations, the gushing spring, the abundant forests, and the beautiful waterfall were all food for many contemplative ruminations, some of which show up in the images used in the gospels.

The only story the gospels record, however, is a momentous one. Mark's Gospel, which is generally regarded as the first to have been written, reports that it was on their visit to Caesarea Philippi that Jesus asked the disciples, "But you—who do you say that I am?" Peter's stark reply, "You are the Messiah" (Mark 8:29) is regarded as a turning point in recognition of Jesus and his mission. "Messiah" is translated as the Christ, the anointed one of God who will bring about the kingdom of God. It is noteworthy that it is not at the Jerusalem temple, the central holy place for Jews, that this turning point is portrayed as taking place. It is far from the center of action, in a place long claimed as sacred by pagans (a term which at that time simply meant, "rustic country people") and more recently occupied by Roman emperor-worshipers, that the flame of faith-insight catches fire.

Matthew elaborates the story further, in ways that will have fateful consequences for the long-term future of Jesus's mission. He portrays Jesus responding to Simon Peter by saying, "You are Peter, and upon this rock I will build my *ekklesia*, and the gates of Hades shall not prevail against it" (Matt16:18). The name Peter, as is well known, means rock in Greek; John 1:42 confirms the renaming of Simon as Cephas, which is Aramaic for rock. Remarkably, in both Mark and Matthew, it is only a few verses after Jesus names Peter "rock" that he calls him "Satan" and an "obstacle" (Mark 8:33; Matt16:23). Whatever it means for Peter to be a rock upon which the church can be built, it evidently does not mean that he has been raised to a superhuman level of rectitude or stability.

If such an exchange really took place at Caesarea Philippi, it is fascinating to think of it occurring in front of the towering rock face of the pagan and imperial shrine. It is as if Jesus is saying, "The real rock upon which I can build is not like this one before which we are standing! Rather, it is that moment of light in which we are united with one another and know one another completely; the moment when you are intimately united with my divine mission and I embrace you in the full truth of who you were created to be. That interpersonal communion of heart between me and you is the foundation of my *ekklesia*, the community of those who will complete my mission. It is because you, Simon Peter, are the first to open yourself to this interior communion of faith that I call you 'rock.' As long as you remain in this communion, you are a rock on which I can build; when you slip away from it, you are an obstacle to me."

Again, we really don't know for sure the historical facts of these events. No one took a video! The story as we have it in the gospels, however, links the crucial awakening of faith-insight to a place with centuries of association to Pan, god of the wild. While Mark does not make any comment beyond identifying the location, there are hints that Matthew is concerned to clarify that communion with Jesus and the nature-based and/or political rituals that took place at places like Caesarea Philippi are not to be equated. In Matthew's version, Jesus's reply to Peter affirms that "It was not flesh and blood that revealed this to you, but my Father in heaven" (Matt 16:17). Another Matthean clarification, perhaps, is in the statement that "the gates of Hades will not prevail" over the power of communion with Jesus. Hades was the abode of the dead, so the meaning seems to be that death will not prevail over those united in the

Heart of Jesus. Caves such as that at Banias were often regarded as entrances to the underworld. "The gates of Hades,"
then, could be another reference to the locale of this inter-
change, and its lack of power in comparison to Jesus.

Still, it is important to remember that Pan was not the god
of Hades or death, but of exuberant, delight-filled life. As for
Jesus, he affirmed that he had come "that they may have life, and
have it in abundance" (John 10:10). This does not mean we can
make a simplistic equation of faith in Christ with ancient fertility
and place-based religions such as those practiced at Paneas. Yet,
as we explore the possibilities of a "new animism" that incultur-
ates Christian faith within what Thomas Berry called the emerging Ecozoic Era, it is essential to take a second look at stories
such as these that offer intriguing fresh perspectives on Jesus's
relation to the old nature-based, indigenous forms of religion.

Relational ontology and deep incarnation

A more systematic approach to re-thinking Jesus from an ecological perspective is offered by some theologians who special-
ize in Christology. Niels Henrik Gregersen was the first to
articulate what he called "deep incarnation," thereby playing
on earlier concepts of "deep ecology" that eliminated anthropocentrism by recognizing the radical interdependence of all
things. As Gregersen expressed it, "My proposal is that the divine Logos (which can be translated as the creative 'Word' or
the formative 'Pattern') has assumed not merely humanity, but
the *whole malleable matrix of materiality*."[1]

Such a perspective is rooted in a relational ontology, which
affirms that organisms and persons—whether human or otherwise

---

1. Niels Henrik Gregersen, "Deep Incarnation: Why Evolutionary Continuity Matters in Christology," *Toronto Journal of Theology* 26, no. 2 (September 2010): 176.

—are not so much separate, individual beings as "a singular locus of creative growth within a continually unfolding field of relationships."[2] Anthropologist Tim Ingold argues that many of the impasses generated by regarding human persons as composites of body-mind-spirit fall away when we take this relational perspective. Humans, like every other creature, dwell in a matrix of relationships and develop needed skills through interacting with all the other beings in the matrix. Ingold adds that in this view, "relations among humans, which we are accustomed to call 'social,' are but a sub-set of ecological relations."[3]

Gregersen's concept of "deep incarnation" plays out the implications of this insight that the physicality of a living being cannot be arbitrarily set apart from the totality of its environment. Any organism's body is completely interdependent with the soil that provides it with nutrients, the water it needs for basic body processes, the gases (e.g., oxygen, carbon dioxide, etc.) that fuel its metabolism, as well as the whole network of other creatures and landscape features within which it finds its habitat and builds its repertoire of skills. All these beings, in turn, participate in other networks of materiality until, ultimately, "the whole malleable matrix of materiality" is implicated in each organism's embodiment.

When we reflect on Jesus as a human being like ourselves, we can (literally) flesh these ideas out Christologically. In chapter 1, we did a thought experiment about taking a video of a year of our life and then playing it back speeded up so that each day passes in a minute. The incessant, rhythmic inward and outward flow of food, water, air, waste products, and bodily detritus reveals the complete interconnection of the human

2. Tim Ingold, *The Perception of the Environment* (Routledge, 2021), 4–5.

3. Ingold, *The Perception of the Environment,* 5.

body with its environment. This illustrates how our body is interdependent with all the global cycles of air, water, and soil, both receiving from them and contributing to them at every moment in time. By affirming that Jesus was a complete human being, we affirm that Jesus too was physically inseparable from the processes of the entire Earth system.

Australian theologian Denis Edwards more fully spelled out the implications of this, writing:

> In the Word made flesh, God is revealed at the heart of the human, and therefore at the heart of all life on Earth. The flesh of Jesus is part of the whole creaturely pattern of life on Earth. When the Word is made flesh, God embraces the long, interconnected history of life in all its complexity and diversity. The incarnation is God-with-us in the "very tissue" of biological life.[4]

Thinking of Jesus in this way, it is easier to see how he is concretely present, involved with, and in relationship with every being in existence. Even in his historical life, during which he was necessarily an individual human being located in a specific and limited place, he was in a more profound sense interconnected with the entire network of life (and minerals, water, soil, etc.) on Earth. Even in the flesh, he was defined less by the boundary of his skin than by the dynamic flow of matter in which he was participant.

Personhood

But what about Christ's "personhood"? Within the first few centuries of the Christian era, the term "person" came to the

---

4. Denis Edwards, *Ecology at the Heart of Faith* (Maryknoll, NY: Orbis Books, 2006), 60.

fore as a key to understanding who Christ was (and is). The issue was how to name what is proper to God without reducing divinity to a dimension of the contingent world. The Greek word *prosopon* (face) and the Latin word *persona* (role) merged into a theological term that refers to a free, incommunicable-yet-communicating, agent of relation. To break that down a bit, a person is free rather than subject to necessity, and incommunicable rather than reducible to graspable materiality. A person constitutively communicates, that is, reaches out beyond the self to share what one has and is; a person is an agent of relation who engages in relationships intentionally, consciously, and wholeheartedly.

A turning point in Christological debates came with the Chalcedonian formula that Christ is "one person in two natures." This formula asserts that Christ is a divine person with both divine and human natures. Even at that time, this was an intellectual brain-breaker, and debate has never ceased on exactly how to spell out what it means.[5] Yet the formula has stuck, persevering like a kind of Rock of Gibraltar through the storms of different philosophical and theological explications of its meaning.

Parallel with these Christological developments, the theology of the Trinity was also coming into focus. Here too the term "person" was seized upon as the key to correct insight. The core statement of Trinitarian doctrine is that God is "three Persons in one God." This is another brain-breaker over which ink has been spilling ever since. The main problem is that if we look to human persons as our model for personhood, this formula of "three persons" would appear to mean that there are

---

5. Brian E. Daley, "Unpacking the Chalcedonian Formula: From Studied Ambiguity to Saving Mystery," *The Thomist* 80, no. 2 (April 2016): 165–89.

three separable individuals and agents, that is, three gods. To maintain the doctrine that there is only one God, we have to understand divine personhood as *sui generis*, that is, it is not reducible to what we observe in human persons.

For human persons, the communion of loving another person can never be absolute; even in the most intense and committed of relationships, each person remains an individual who potentially can separate from the other, whether willingly or unwillingly. In divine personhood, however, radical communion is constitutive. The three persons draw upon a single font of uncreated divine communion as they each present their unique faces within creation. Thus, biblical scholars can find textual grounding to sketch out distinct "personalities" and behavioral profiles for Father, Son, and Holy Spirit, while still confirming that biblical faith never deviates from absolute monotheism.

The realization that then emerges is that from a theological (rather than psychological) perspective, human personhood is an image of divine personhood rather than the other way around. While the human capacities for personal agency, interiority, intimacy, and self-giving are finite, they are nonetheless a created participation in the infinite and uncreated personal life of God. One of the clues to this is how we humans are always longing and seeking to expand our freedom, knowledge, self-possession, and love. We never stop longing for infinity, even as we are so frequently reminded of our finitude.

A question that has become prominent in recent decades is whether the category of personhood should be extended beyond divine and human beings. This is being debated in many secular fields such as philosophy, psychology, and zoology, as well as in theology. Traditionally the assumption has been that human beings are categorically persons, regardless of manifested abilities, while animals or other creatures are not—

again, regardless of manifested abilities. The challenge is that if we define personhood in terms such as self-awareness, intentional action, or free self-giving, it seems that some human beings (e.g., infants, the mentally disabled, those suffering from severe dementia) would not qualify. Meanwhile, zoological research daily discovers more and more of these or similar abilities in at least some animals.

In the traditional view that limits personhood to humans, being a person is something like belonging to a species. A ringtailed lemur can be identified as a member of that species, even if it is born without a tail, is unusually small or large, or in other ways does not fit the norms of the species. A mongoose lemur is not a ring-tailed lemur, even if (unusually) it is born with rings on its tail or in other ways resembles its sister species. In this view, humans are the only earthly members of the species "persons." Even if some animals exhibit what we regard as human-like abilities, they cannot be considered persons.

Defending this assumption requires at least tacit acceptance of a hierarchical view of the world, a view that posits a series of clear lines of demarcation distinguishing God from humans, humans from animals, animals from vegetation, and vegetation from non-living matter. However, this way of thinking about personhood seems like a category mistake. Personhood cannot really be defined by whether something exhibits a specified set of characteristics, but rather by how it participates in the very being of God. Everything created by God, it seems, must participate in God's being in some way.

Actually, it is not particularly radical to say that all created beings manifest something of the being of God. Bonaventure is an example of a medieval theologian who had a hierarchical theory of how created things manifest the being of God: all things are shadows of God; living creatures are vestiges of God, rational creatures are images of God, and those who conform to God's will are likenesses of God. While attractive, such a hierarchical view is problematic, both scientifically and theologically. Evolution has shown that all life, whether animal, plant, fungi, or microbe, has emerged from a single original source. Even the line between living and non-living is not clear, with questions about which side viruses belong on. It would be more accurate to say that the only truly clear line of demarcation is that between God and creation—and that has been breached by the incarnation!

Giving and receiving gifts

This is the context in which we reconsider the potential value of an animistic viewpoint. One of the most widely recognized scholars of animism, Graham Harvey, defines it as "engagement with a world that is full of persons, only some of whom are human."[6] In the animistic worldview, persons (whether human or not) "are those with whom other persons interact with varying degrees of reciprocity.... Persons are volitional, relational, cultural, and social beings. They demonstrate intentionality and agency with varying degrees of autonomy and freedom."[7] Animists, then, perceive personhood, and the possibility of personal relationship, as potential within many aspects of the created world rather than as being confined to humans and human relationships.

How this actually plays out differs considerably among the hundreds of indigenous animist worldviews. In a famous essay written more than fifty years ago, ethnographer Irving Hallowell asked an Anishinaabe (Ojibwa) elder whether all

---

6. Graham Harvey, *Animism: Respecting the Living World*, 2nd ed., revised and updated (London: Hurst & Company, 2017), xviii.

7. Harvey, *Animism*, xvii.

the stones they saw around them were alive. The elder paused, then answered "No, but some of them are."[8] Further probing revealed that the difference is that while most stones are just stones, some stones understand what is said to them and respond actively. In this elder's view, the same may be true of some animals, trees, mountains, bodies of water, and so on. As Graham Harvey spells it out more fully, for the animist any being may engage in a personal relationship if it knows how to give and receive gifts. In an animist perspective, then, personhood is a question not of the nature of a thing but of its "etiquette and ethics. Finding the appropriate local way to share, to give, and to receive gifts, is what makes someone recognizable as a person."[9]

I do not have the expertise to spell out exactly what the gift-giving of a stone is like in the experience of an Anishinaabe person. However, the experience I recounted at the beginning of this chapter gives me fodder for speculation on what it could mean in a "new animist" perspective. That day, "walking with lemur," the sky and water and greenery and birdsong all seemed to unfold as one great holy gift. In that case it was not so much a single stone that sparkled, but all of them. When one is at one with the world, everything seems to communicate with your soul. Nothing was spoken in words, yet I felt as if each creature was giving me gifts of wisdom.

For example, I was stopped in my tracks by the twisted, crumbling, wildly intricate profile of a dead stump at the side of the path. Drawing closer, I found a young tree growing from

8. A. Irving Hallowell, "Ojibwa Ontology, Behavior, and World View," in *Culture in History: Essays in Honor of Paul Radin*, ed. Stanley Diamond (New York: Columbia University Press, 1960), 19–52.

9. Graham Harvey, "If Not All Stones Are Alive...: Radical Relationality in Animism Studies," *Journal for the Study of Religion, Nature and Culture* 11, no. 4 (October 2017): 493.

the side of what appeared to be thoroughly rotten wood. The young tree looked strong, straight, and healthy. A little farther along, I began to examine a different tree with two unusual round, smooth burls embedded in its trunk. At eye level, the tree looked quite firm and robust. When I twisted my head to look up through all the branches and leaves, however, I realized that this particular tree was dead—and probably had been for some time. A deeper wisdom about life and death than I could have learned by taking several courses on the subject had lodged in my soul as a result of my interaction with these trees.

Accepting the idea that stones or trees can communicate requires significant adjustments to our standard Western worldview. In *How Forests Think*, Eduardo Kohn develops the viewpoint that all things are communicating, all of the time. Grasses (and all other plants) intricately interpret and interact with changing conditions of soil, fungi, water, sun, insects, and pollutants in order to enhance their survival and reproduction.[10] A flower deploys its odors, colors, shapes, and movements to communicate with sunlight, insects, animals, and even other plants. It makes adjustments in response to whatever beings and conditions show up. When we invite a plant to flourish by offering it different conditions of sunlight, water, nutrients, or companion plants, we are making an effort to communicate in the plant's own language. Yet we rarely provide the plants that give us so much pleasure with the full range of conditions in which they can reproduce effectively. The more we make the effort to learn all the subtleties of the plant's language, the more we may become truly a participant in its world—the world in which it flourishes by interacting wisely and effectively with all the creatures that surround it.

---

10. Eduardo Kohn, *How Forests Think: Toward an Anthropology beyond the Human* (Berkeley: University of California Press, 2013), 34.

Most humans have some awareness that animals communicate through sounds, silences, gestures, movement, coloration, built structures, and more. Our ability to understand and communicate with them, however, tends to be severely limited by self-interest. We know that if we put seed in a bird-feeder, birds will come so we can enjoy watching them. We have learned that we can spray rabbit repellent on our garden plants so the bunnies won't come near them. We have even trained service dogs to detect problematic physiological changes and alert us. Yet most of the ways in which other creatures seek to interact with their surroundings are completely lost on us.

Many animals and insects, for example, hear and respond to sounds in ranges that have no impact on us. Our noses miss most of the smells that a dog expertly picks up. Our attention, not surprisingly, focuses on human language and ways of communicating, so that we may notice a written placard telling us a tree's species but pay little attention to the subtleties of what the tree actually looks, smells, feels, and sounds like. As David Toolan puts it, "The universe is a gigantic communications network, a complex circuitry of instructions, most of which we can barely decipher."[11] We miss most of the communications of the matrix of beings within which we live because we are clueless about how to exchange gifts with them.

The "personing" of Christ

The more profound meaning of the chapter's title, "Christ of the Forest," is that Christ, whose very identity is to be the Heart at the heart of the world, lives, communicates, and gifts us with

---

11. David Toolan, *At Home in the Cosmos* (Maryknoll, NY: Orbis Books, 2001), 183.

grace from the heart of every wild thing in the vast matrix of this Earthly community of beings within which we are grown into existence. Another story can help to bring this idea to life.

On a retreat near the seashore, I went out for a walk on a very hot day. Clambering with considerable effort over large piles of stones, I imprudently went a long way down the rocky shoreline before I realized how worn out and overheated I had become. As I turned to make my way back, I felt groggy and began to worry that I might be getting heatstroke. The rock piles went on and on with no shade in sight, and I still had a long way to go to get back to my starting point. Then, one very large rock a little farther away from the shoreline seemed to beckon me. As I approached it I saw that on its far side there was a small, cave-like area of shadow where I could ensconce myself. Slipping into the cool shade, I relaxed with deep relief and gratitude.

As I lay there, a Bible verse came into my head: "I will put you in a cleft of the rock, and will cover you with my hand until I have passed by" (Exod 33:22). To be sure, the verse did not exactly describe my situation, as my context was totally different from that of Moses. Nonetheless, I physically felt the saving gift of the "cleft of the rock," extended just in the nick of time. My tradition and my faith context attributed the gift, ultimately, to God; yet as a physical experience, the gift came from the rock, which had seemed to beckon me and which then provided a cool, embracing space exactly the right size for my body. In fact, it was Christ-in-the-rock that I encountered that day.

I began to reflect on this in fresh ways after I participated in an online training program with the Association of Nature and Forest Therapy Guides to become a Forest Therapy guide.[12] The practice of Forest Therapy originated in Japan in

---

12. Association of Nature & Forest Therapy Guides and Programs, https://www.natureandforesttherapy.earth/.

the 1980s, when health professionals realized that a profound cause of stress for modern city dwellers is their almost complete lack of contact with anything natural or wild. The Japanese called the practice *Shinrin-yoku*, or "Forest Bathing." Forest Therapy is a way of guiding people toward availability for a profound encounter with the creatures and features of the natural world. Exactly what each participant will experience is not prescribed, but in fact almost all participants report surprised delight in their unique encounter. Sometimes these encounters are really life changing. Put in the terms of the new animism, many people (who are, obviously, steeped in modern Western ways) are surprised to discover a personal and deeply meaningful relationship with a tree, or insect, or pond, or sunlight, or other creature.

As I have led groups in Forest Therapy, the insight that has slowly begun to emerge for me is that since Christ is at the heart of relationality in all creation, he can awaken and inhabit that personal relationality in the rock, tree, insect, or pond in its encounter with a human person. It dawned on me that this may best be expressed in a verb, "to person." Christ's personhood permeates the created world and may emerge anywhere as "personing." To "person" is to emerge as a center of active and intimate relationship. Persons only emerge *in* relationship; there are no persons if they are not actively personing. Christ, as the one who is in active and intimate relationship with the entire creation, is able to person anywhere and anytime. One might say that he *is* the principle of creation's ability to person.

In his *New Seeds of Contemplation*, Thomas Merton says something similar but uses a more impersonal metaphor. Observing that "[God's] truth and [God's] love pervade all things as the light and heat of the sun pervade our atmosphere," he adds that, "as a magnifying glass concentrates the rays of the sun into a little burning knot of heat that can set fire to a dry leaf or a piece of paper, so the mystery of Christ in the Gospel concentrates the rays of God's light and fire to a point that sets fire to the [human] spirit."[13] My suggestion is that the metaphor of "personing" is even more apt; Christ's personal love pervades all creation, and so can, by grace, emerge as a "little burning knot" of intensified personal love manifested through any created thing, at any time.

As we approach the end of this chapter, let us return once more to the story of Jesus and his disciples at Caesarea Philippi. We recall that when Jesus called Peter "rock," he seemed to be referring to the foundation of intimate communion with Jesus that enabled Peter to know Jesus's true identity. In other words, Jesus "personed" in Peter; he awakened in him the radical fullness of personal relationship, and Peter recognized that event as the salvation of God. This is a way of understanding our most significant religious experiences of encounter with Christ.

Many experiences of personing in the natural world, however, are not explicitly connected with Christianity or any other religion. Thus, we cannot presume that anyone having such an experience of some aspect of the wild world reaching out to embrace them at a deep personal level will automatically go from there to affirming Jesus in the way Peter did. Yet we can also recall what Paul said in Romans 1:20: "From the creation of the world, God's invisible qualities, eternal power and divine nature, have been clearly observed in what God made." God's personhood, consisting of infinite capacity for intimate and loving relationship, is potential in every created thing. While practices like Forest Therapy, as such, are not aimed at

---

13. Thomas Merton, *New Seeds of Contemplation* (New York: New Directions, 2007), 150–51.

preaching the gospel, perhaps in an appropriate setting one could invite participants to discover the connection between the soul-enlivening experience they have had in their encounters with other-than-human beings and the person of Christ, who is implicit wherever "personing" occurs.

Conclusion: Spirit and spirits

More traditionally, the capacity of God to manifest freely anywhere in creation has been identified more with the Holy Spirit than with Christ. Christian orthodoxy affirms that there is only one God, and that where one of the three divine Persons is, the others necessarily are as well, so on a practical level this distinction may not matter greatly. The essential concept is that the animistic sense of real personal relationship emergent anywhere in the more-than-human world has a theological basis. However, the language of "Spirit" may be more amenable for some, especially those who do not identify as Christian.

Spirit-language also makes a more direct connection to the animistic language of "spirits." As Swedish theologian Sigurd Bergmann affirms, animism and its talk of spirits need not be seen as the opposite of belief in the Spirit, but rather as a mode of belief in the radical life-giving character of God. In this view, he writes, "spirits are not regarded as pagan counter-beings but as co-workers with, and guardians of, the Holy Spirit; spiritual animations of natural life forms are not seen as simply superstitious and magic but as valuable cultural skills to make oneself at home in Creation with the Spirit and to restore our home, the Earth, in synergy with her."[14] In the next chapter, we

---

14. Sigurd Bergmann, "Life-Giving Breath: Ecological Pneumatology in the Context of Fetishization," *The Ecumenical Review* 65, no. 1 (March 2013): 209, https://doi.org/10.1111/erev.12030.

will explore more deeply some of these "skills" that enable us to live more fully and responsibly in the community of Earth, our "common home."

FOR REFLECTION AND PRACTICE:

Has a stone ever given you a gift? How about a wild animal, or a tree, or a mountain? What can it mean to exchange gifts with wild and natural beings?

In whom or what have you experienced Christ "personing"? Or, is it easier for you to think of these encounters using the language of "Spirit"?

FOR FURTHER READING:

Denis Edwards, *Jesus the Wisdom of God: An Ecological Theology* (Eugene, OR: Wipf & Stock, 2005).

Belden C. Lane, *The Great Conversation: Nature and the Care of the Soul* (New York: Oxford University, 2019).

Robert Shore-Goss, *God Is Green: An Eco-spirituality of Incarnate Compassion* (Eugene, OR: Cascade, 2016).

7

YOKED HEARTS

What kind of relationship is possible with the Heart of God, here and now? This is a different question than that explored in a previous chapter, which looked at some of Jesus's relationships during the time when he walked on Earth. Once Jesus's earthly life had ended, some ways of relating were foreclosed while others opened up. Part of the hypothesis being explored in this book is that, since the Heart at the heart of the world can "person" anywhere and in anything, heartful relationship is not limited only to explicitly Christian contexts. For Christians, however, that is where we begin.

Take up my yoke

Meditating on Matthew 11:29, "Take my yoke upon you and learn from me, for I am gentle and humble in heart," I imagine myself walking beside Jesus like an ox companionably pulling a load together with another ox. Jesus is the lead "ox," keeping me calm as he gently shows me the way. The humility of the image is touching; Jesus places himself beside me as fellow cart-puller, rather than in the role of master or driver. This meditation opens up a deep sense of intimacy and companionship. I feel my heart yoked with that of Jesus, and I feel a great openness to learning in the presence of this gentle and humble guide.

The image of being yoked together at the heart is a tender and powerful expression of the Christian's faith relationship with Jesus. It is an image of partnership and mutuality, as those walking side by side share the load in whatever tasks they seek to accomplish. It is also an image of fidelity through thick and thin, as the committed companions do not abandon one another even when stressful events make it difficult to give much direct attention to the relationship. The two participate wholeheartedly in all aspects of each other's lives and experiences. Within the Christian framework, one "ox" is the disciple of the other; yet this is a discipleship of companionship, not of command.

Interiority and participation

The yoking of hearts is an interior experience. Often, the Western tendency to dualism makes what is going on "inside" of our minds and hearts and what is going on in "the real world" into parallel tracks that may intersect or even briefly join together at certain points, but are more fundamentally separate. This chapter explores a very different perspective. It is expressed by David Abram when he writes: "What if there is, yes, a quality of inwardness to the mind, not because the mind is located inside us (inside our body or brain), but because we are situated, bodily *inside* it—because our lives and our thoughts unfold in the depths of a mind that is not really ours, but is rather the Earth's?"[1]

When we remain in the more typical assumption that our consciousness is "inside" and separate from the world around

---

1. David Abram, *Becoming Animal: An Earthly Cosmology* (New York: Vintage, 2010), 123.

us, the admonition that it is essential to cultivate a deep interior life is sometimes interpreted as encouraging an attitude of not caring about anything except one's "special" inward experiences. The critique that an intensive focus on interior spirituality can put one at risk of becoming disconnected from relationships, practical life, and action for social justice is not completely without merit. Still, the insistence that this must always be the case is based in a fundamental misrepresentation of the authentic character of interiority.

Although the language of interiority may sound like "staring inward," its real meaning is being alive and present from the core of one's existence. Primordially, we are born immersed in what Andreas Weber calls "the unfathomably complex relatedness that lies at the foundation of all things."[2] The original experience of being alive is pure intersubjectivity, pure belonging-with-as-one. Robert Sardello names this "heartfulness," writing: "By becoming what we are present with—through the rhythms of our body, intensified most completely within the heart—we know by communion rather than by the distance of mental-ness." Heartful contemplative presence, he continues,

> simultaneously beholds, embraces, and enlivens whatever we come into contact with, be it ourselves, others, nature, and even "things." . . . As soon as we touch into heart, we find ourselves in intimate relation with invisible "presences." We do not navigate the primordial currents of the rhythms of the heart alone. In fact, the most immediate, the most given sense of being within the heart consists of heart-as-holy-relation.[3]

2. Andreas Weber, *Matter and Desire: An Erotic Ecology* (White River Junction, VT: Chelsea Green Publishing, 2017), 120.

3. Robert Sardello, *Heartfulness* (Gainesville, TX: Goldenstone Press, 2015), 5, 8, 22.

As we grow through all the stages of life, that foundational intersubjectivity has to mature from the infant's relatively oblivious narcissism, which assumes that everything is here to serve oneself, into responsible love. The capacity to love responsibly requires full development of both interior self-presence and receptivity to the (exterior) other. In actual love, these two flow in and through one another, so that the one who loves both dwells in the other and embraces the other all in one paradoxical movement. Weber summarizes: "Because love is the site where inner and outer dimensions meet and mutually comprehend one another, there is an ineluctable feedback loop between the way we treat the world and the depths of our love." Accurately understood, interiority is not solipsistic, but the participatory foundation of all responsible action.

The mature, authentic interiority of the heart that spiritual teachers laud means completely surrendering into relationship with divine Heart as the foundation of one's existence. This is how the Flemish mystic Jan Ruusbroec (1293–1381) describes it: "God's touch and his giving of himself, together with our striving in love and our giving of ourselves in return—this is what sets love on a firm foundation. This flux and reflux make the spring of love overflow, so that God's touch and our striving in love become a single love."[4] In another place, Ruusbroec adds that such a one will always "flow forth to all who need him." Thus, this fully mature person will lead what Ruusbroec calls "a common life," meaning that they are "equally ready for contemplation or for action and perfect in both."[5]

---

4. Jan van Ruusbroec, *John Ruusbroec: The Spiritual Espousals and Other Works*, The Classics of Western Spirituality (Mahwah, NJ: Paulist Press, 1985), 115.

5. Ruusbroec, *John Ruusbroec.*

Ecology of mind and imagination

While the Christian's relationship with Jesus is unique, then, the bonding of hearts is not. In fact, there is a sense in which such a bond is the most basic process of all life. All matter, from the smallest particles to the most complex living creatures, has an innate tendency to form attachments to others. Andreas Weber names this as a fundamentally erotic orientation at the heart of being. *Eros*, as Doug Christie notes, is simply the inbuilt and universal longing to share in the life of another, and it is increasingly being recognized as a core dimension of the natural world as well as of human participation in that world.[6] As Weber puts it, "Life is touch in a much deeper sense than just touching skin to skin, colliding against foreign masses: It is touch as penetration of one by another. The existence of each one of us—plants, animal cells, I as a human being—depends solely on the mutual relatedness manifested in this exchange."[7]

The yoking together of hearts and of bodies (not just sexually, but in many configurations of shared life) is central for the survival and flourishing of life, both individual and communal. As humans, we are vitally attached not only to other humans, but to microbes, animals, trees, bodies of water, soils, landscapes, and seasonal changes, to name only a few. Some of these attachments are conscious, but if we look beyond consciousness we glimpse the myriad root-hairs of our deep being as they draw nourishment from the wild, fermenting web of tiny unseen creatures whose digestion constantly performs alchemy on flakes of matter. Long before we can even begin to

---

6. Douglas E. Christie, *The Blue Sapphire of the Mind: Notes for a Contemplative Ecology* (Oxford, UK: Oxford University Press, 2013), 227.

7. Weber, *Matter and Desire*, 57.

envision taking up the yoke of discipleship, we are already intimately yoked to a complex ecosystem of large and small creatures—both human and more-than-human—whose lives and ours are mutually interdependent.

While modern Westerners rarely have deep awareness of this body-and-soul interconnection with the land we inhabit, many indigenous cultures live wholly from this perspective. They experience themselves as physically, mentally, and spiritually rooted in a home-place that knows them intimately and that they know intimately. These roots are not merely here and now, but reach back through deep time to "forever." The land and creatures of this place are constantly communicating with the people, providing them with the guidance they need to be faithful in creating a future where human, animal, and plant nations can continue to flourish. A core assumption in this worldview is that if people are listening, natural creatures and phenomena genuinely are communicating with them. Here is how native Hawaiian Adin Kawate explains it:

> I was taught by a Hawaiian man I consider an uncle and mentor. "The spirit of God is in the rock, the plant, the cloud, the mountain and the ocean," he said.

> From Uncle, I learned that Hawaiians were a people of prayer. It was the simplest ritual to connect with Spirit. They prayed all the time and in all situations.

> . . .

> Here is a truth I learned from Indigenous mentors: If you connect with the Spirit in the rock, you now have a relationship with the rock. If you connect with the Spirit in the tree, you now have a relationship with the tree. It is the same with the cloud, same with the mountain, same with the ocean.

> And you join in on the thousands-of-years-old conversation.

And how do you know you are conversing? Natural phenomena. Hoʻailona.[8]

In Kawate's culture, then, the particular hue of the sunset,
the distant hooting of a pueo (Hawaiian owl), or the shape of
a stone on the seashore may carry a message for the listener's
soul. Haudenosaunee scholar Roronhiakewen Dan Longboat
calls this thinking with an "old-growth mind."[9] He contrasts it
with the "settler mind" of those of us who do not feel our visceral
rootedness in any particular place. Settlers regard the stories and
myths that emerge from the indigenous "thousands-of-years-
old conversation" as mere imagination. For the settler, imagination is something one can play with to create futures totally
disconnected from the vast web of delicate interconnections
upon which one actually feeds. For the old-growth mind, in
contrast, imagination "is the cognitive and spiritual condition
of entwining with local and cosmological intelligences.... [It]
is a homing device for finding a way into the sacred unity of
time, mind, spirit, and place."[10]

In fact, Longboat prefers not even to use the tainted word
"imagination" but instead to speak of the "ecology of mind."
Human mind itself is an evolutionary emergent of the "thousands-
of-years-old conversation" of the vast web of created beings.
Indigenous wisdom, he notes, affirms that "Humans think at

---

8. Adin Kawate, "Huli Lua E," *Humans and Nature Stories* (blog), ac-
cessed December 9, 2022, https://humansandnature.org/huli-lua-e/.

9. Joe Sheridan and Roronhiakewen "He Clears the Sky" Dan Longboat, "The Haudenosaunee Imagination and the Ecology of the Sacred,"
Space and Culture 9, no. 4 (2006): 365–81, https://doi.org/10.1177/
1206331206292503.

10. Sheridan and Longboat, "The Haudenosaunee Imagination," 370,
375.

their best if they know they are the last beings created."[11] Since creation and mind are expressions of each other, they have a mutual interest in forming a deep friendship. Only if humans are faithful to this friendship by "minding Creation" will the spiritual helpers "look after a human vulnerability dependent on all the other creatures, birds, trees, plants, and insects."[12] What the settlers call imagination, the indigenous regard as the sacred communication of the ancient community of life, without whose assistance humanity is doomed.

Dreams, visions, and shamanic journeys

For indigenous peoples, dreams, visions, and shamanic journeys are all ways in which the cosmos communicates with human beings. What all of these phenomena share in common is that they involve vividly imaged stories that take place in a human mind without being intentionally created by that mind. They are different from fantasies, which are instigated and governed by the conscious mind. Certain intentional practices and techniques can be employed to invite dreams, visions, and shamanic journeys, but it is only by surrendering to a liminal state in which the conscious mind relinquishes control that they occur. Most indigenous cultures enshrine one or more of these practices as sacred ways of welcoming the guidance of the deep web of life within which they live. For them, human bodies and souls—like those of all creatures— are permeable in their roots to the ever-murmuring sea of communications that constitutes the universe. When one enters a liminal state of openness to this communication, the images

---

11. Sheridan and Longboat, "The Haudenosaunee Imagination," 359.

12. Sheridan and Longboat, "The Haudenosaunee Imagination," 374.

and stories that appear in the mind are not random; they are holy guidance.

Western psychology, in contrast, names the source of dream imagery as "the unconscious," which is regarded as a dangerous, unruly locale in our individual psyches that holds both the repressed and the untamed (mainly sexual) energies that have never been integrated by the controlling ego. In this view, the unconscious is the seamy underbelly of the individual psyche. The only messages the "wild" imagery of dreams and similar phenomena may hold for us are those about our individual pathologies. While occasionally people may spontaneously experience a "spiritual" dream that holds great significance for them, nothing in the culture prepares for or encourages this. On the contrary, the general attitude is that dreams are nothing more than the bizarre play of the psyche, best allowed to fade away as quickly as possible into the practical light of day.

As for visions, these are regarded with even greater suspicion. The fear in this case is that they represent either the complete fragmentation of the central self, or the meddling of foreign agents (demons) with evil intent. Both of these fears are based, again, in the assumption that the human being is an individual, separate being for whom the breach of the boundaries of separateness is fundamentally dangerous. It is common to hear religious visions lumped together with the pathological "voices" heard by some people with certain types of mental illness. The emphasis of modern Western culture on the primacy of ego-control and conscious, rational thought marginalizes visions, regarding them as far more likely to be malignant than therapeutic.

Shamanic journeying is not well known in the Western world, although neo-shamanism—which promotes a modernized form of shamanic journey for urbanized, non-indigenous people—is a fast-growing movement. Indigenous shamans generally do not choose their role, but receive a calling that is confirmed by other members of their community. They often undergo an initiation process that involves a harrowing journey to the "underworld" where they experience violent dismemberment and then are reborn. Their role in their community is to be the local expert at soliciting and receiving guidance from animals, ancestors, guiding spirits, and cosmic forces. This is typically done through ritualized journeys to the underworld and/or the "upper world" where they meet and interact with these guides.

From the point of view of an observer, shamans often appear to be in a kind of trance during their journeys. From the shaman's point of view, however, they are moving through florid landscapes and encountering all sorts of beings, most of whom take the shape of animals or what Westerners would call mythological creatures. The best analogy is perhaps a vivid dream that one experiences as completely real as long as one is immersed in it. Most of the information that traditional indigenous shamans sought in these journeys was very practical; for example, how and where to find the animals or plants the community needed for food, or how to resolve conflicts within the community or with others. In the more modernized neo-shamanic movement, people are more often seeking guidance related to personal issues rather than on behalf of their communities.

One can compare the indigenous understanding of the imaginal world to the life cycle of a mushroom. What we identify as a mushroom is its fruiting body, which is often quite small and visible for only a short time. The fibers of the fungal mycelia, however, can branch out through the surrounding soil for several kilometers in every direction. Invisible underneath the surface, the mycelia continuously exchange nutrients with many varieties of microbes as well as with the roots of numerous plants and trees. The health of the whole ecosystem is dependent upon these multitudinous subterranean relationships. Similarly, the dream or vision that comes forth in a seer's mind is fleeting, but it is the "fruiting body" of the entire invisible network of communicating beings that the seer inhabits. Receptiveness to the communication in the dream or vision is essential for the flourishing of both humans and all those others, visible and invisible, with whom they are in symbiotic relationship.

In indigenous cultures, the reception and interpretation of these imaginal messages take place within traditions of practice and discernment that have been developed over hundreds or perhaps thousands of generations. Thus, for modern Westerners the turn toward openness to these deep Earth-rooted communications will not be so simple as just paying attention to dreams or eliminating one's prejudice against visions. In fact, naïve, untutored receptivity to imaginal eruptions clearly can have many dangers. Western culture is currently in the throes of an epidemic of bizarre conspiracy theories and anti-science activism, so it is hardly the time to toss out all our Western-developed traditions of fact-checking and practical reason. Yet the evident ill health of both the Earth and our human societies—manifested in skyrocketing rates of depression, anxiety, and suicide, especially among the young—begs for us to begin the long and difficult process of recalibrating our ways of thinking and being toward a newly humbled consciousness of our interdependence with the whole Earthly web of life. One element of this needs to be renewed openness to exploring these ancient ways of knowing and communicating with the more-than-human world.

A new shamanism

In his 1988 book *The Dream of the Earth*, Passionist priest Thomas Berry lifted up the urgent need for modern Westerners to reclaim what he called "the shamanic personality." He wrote:

> The shamanic personality speaks and best understands the language of the various creatures of the earth.... This shamanic insight is especially important just now when history is being made not primarily within nations or between nations, but between humans and the earth—with all its living creatures. In this context all our professions and institutions must be judged primarily by the extent to which they foster this mutually enhancing human-earth relationship.[13]

Somewhat similarly, the Sri Lankan Buddhist anthropologist Gananath Obeyesekere called for a revival of ancient ways of knowing through intuition, visions, aphoristic thinking, and dreams. He wrote: "As I see it, some of our profoundest insights of the spirit emerge from processes of thought outside the rational cogito."[14] Like Berry, he argued that only an alliance between this pre-rational visionary knowledge and more ego-controlled reason can bring forth the kind of wisdom needed in our time.

While some practitioners such as Michael Harner and Sandra Ingerman have successfully repackaged shamanic journeying so as to introduce it to many who have no ancestral or personal connection to indigenous traditions, it still appears

---

13. Thomas Berry, *The Dream of the Earth*, reprint (Berkeley, CA: Counterpoint, 2015), 211–12.

14. Gananath Obeyesekere, *The Awakened Ones: Phenomenology of Visionary Experience* (New York: Columbia University Press, 2012), 474.

foreign or even bizarre to most modern Westerners. How, then, can the Earth-rooted wisdom, healing, and reconciliation that traditional shamanism and similar practices represent be made more broadly accessible today?

In view of answering that question, Sister of Saint Joseph Toni Nash has articulated four principles of the shamanic worldview.[15] These are what remain constant, even when the practices and accoutrements of shamanic practice change substantially. The principles are:

1. Everything in the world is alive, with an interiority and a spiritual consciousness that can communicate. All beings are interconnected from within. The shaman lives in the intimacy of this community.

2. Everything consists of the energy initiated at the origin of creation. This energy is constantly evolving and transforming. The shaman is able to enter a state of awareness of the movement of this energy.

3. The entire universe is sacred, and has purpose and meaning. Everything in it is to be respected as a subject responsible for its own evolution toward greater complexity and consciousness. The shaman bonds with these mysteries and powers of the universe.

4. The natural world provides us with the most direct and immediate experience of spirit. Through it, we can access the healing power of the spirit world. The shaman knows how to receive these energies and direct them toward healing and harmony.

---

15. Toni Nash, "Shamanism and Cosmogenesis," Sisters of Earth conference on Shamanic Wisdom, July 15, 2022.

Sister of Charity Mary Bookser is another woman religious who has been trained in shamanic practices. When asked about the uneasiness some Christians feel about the term "shamanism," she commented: "Shamanism is just a word."[16] We do not necessarily have to call this exploration of new ways of knowing "shamanism," nor should we assume that the only way to engage in it is by embracing traditional shamanic practice with its ceremonies, near-death experiences, underworld or upper world journeys, animal and spirit guides, and so on. Some will find those practices helpful, while others will do better with other means such as poetry, chanting, journaling, guided imagery, contemplative time in nature, and so on. What matters is finding ways to grow in the worldview expressed in the principles Nash articulates, while integrating it with our Christian faith.

Wisdom as participation

It is in the theology of Wisdom that all this can come together. In the Bible, the wisdom literature is a diverse genre that focuses on right relationships among people, God, and the natural world. Rather than placing emphasis on where things fit within the great narrative of salvation history, wisdom literature focuses more on creation and everyday life as the locales where God is manifest. Seeking a conjunction between these biblical traditions and current scientific practice, Jeffrey Schloss defines wisdom as "living in a way that corresponds to how things are. It is not mere knowledge, nor is it mere moral admonition, but it involves deep insight into the functioning, meaning, and purposes of existence along with the ability to

---

16. Mary Bookser, SC, Sisters of Earth Zoom workshop, February 17, 2022.

discern how to live accordingly, that is, in accord with the way things are."[17]

Sergei Bulgakov (1871–1944) was a Russian Orthodox priest and theologian who sought to develop a refreshed Sophiology (theology of Wisdom). He envisioned Wisdom as the ebullient erotic longing of God—the love that gushes infinitely in the love among Father, Son, and Holy Spirit and then pours into creation and incarnation. As Christopher Pramuk summarizes, it is Wisdom "that 'opens room' in God's very self for all the world, from the beginning."[18] Wisdom, according to Bulgakov, is that primordial maternal matrix from which all things, whether galaxies or mountains or microbes or human beings, spring forth trailing divine splendor. Thus, it is by apprenticing ourselves to Wisdom that we may learn to live as participants in God's very self.

In the section of his gospel where he offers the metaphor of the "yoke," Matthew portrays Jesus as both the new Moses and personified Wisdom.[19] Both are figures of humility, intimacy with God, and communal guidance. The "take up my yoke" text that we reflected on at the beginning of this chapter echoes Sirach 51:26, "Put your neck under her [wisdom's] yoke, and let your soul receive instruction." For Christians, it is in being

---

17. Jeffrey Schloss, "Wisdom Traditions as Mechanisms for Organismal Integration: Evolutionary Perspectives on Homeostatic 'Laws of Life,'" in *Understanding Wisdom: Sources, Science and Society*, ed. Warren S. Brown, Laws of Life Symposia Series, vol. 3 (Philadelphia: Templeton Foundation Press, 2000), 157.

18. Christopher Pramuk, "Wisdom, Our Sister: Thomas Merton's Reception of Russian Sophiology," *Spiritus: A Journal of Christian Spirituality* 11, no. 2 (2011): 181, https://doi.org/10.1353/scs.2011.0045.

19. Patricia Sharbaugh, "The New Moses and the Wisdom of God: A Convergence of Themes in Matthew 11:25–30," *Horizons* 40, no. 2 (December 2013): 199–217, https://doi.org/10.1017/hor.2013.78.

yoked to Jesus—that is, by being in intimate relationship with him and with everything he is in relationship to—that we learn wisdom. True wisdom, then, is participatory and relational. One could memorize reams of wisdom sayings so as to be able to pass a test, but gain little wisdom. It is the one who may know few of the sayings but is yoked at the heart to the Heart of God who is wise.

Living wisely, then, demands that we shift the epistemological assumptions that have been firmly in place for centuries if not longer. A relational approach essentially means affirming that the ground of deep knowledge is participatory rather than objectifying. Things are known most fully in the context of meaningful engagement with them within their total environment of relations. Thus, I know the tree outside my window most truly when it and its relationships (to wind, soil, birds, insects, etc.) are woven meaningfully into my own life and relationships. The ability to distance oneself and objectify is a secondary skill that always must be referred back to the ground of participation.

The more typical Western position has been the opposite: since the tree is merely material and completely separate from me and my mind, I know it best when I set aside its meaning or interest to myself and study it objectively. When such a dualistic epistemology, which separates matter from mind or spirit, is enshrined as primary rather than embedded within a more foundational participatory epistemology, it has proven to lead to the disastrous consequence of profound destruction of the habitats of humans and multitudes of other living things. As Stephan Harding puts it, science has made us clever, but not wise. We will find wisdom, he suggests, "by replacing our demonstrably unwise (and until recently, unconscious) assumption that the world is an inert machine with the arguably wiser and more accurate metaphor of the world as a vast animate (and hence 'sentient') being."[20] This is the perspective that is also at the basis of the "new animism,"[21] which we discussed in chapter 3.

Affirming a similar position in the 1970s, Gregory Bateson proposed that since the human mind is interconnected with all beings in its roots, it innately has the capacity to tap into the "thousands-of-years-long conversation" among all created beings. He wrote:

> The cybernetic epistemology which I have offered you would suggest a new approach. The individual mind is immanent but not only in the body. It is immanent also in pathways and messages outside the body; and there is a larger mind of which the individual mind is only a sub-system. This larger Mind is comparable to God and is perhaps what some people mean by "God," but it is still immanent in the total interconnected social system and planetary ecology.[22]

Although Bateson did not identify this "larger mind" explicitly with the biblical image of Holy Wisdom, his perspective offers a redolent clue to how we might think Wisdom afresh. Elizabeth A. Johnson's concept of Wisdom as "unimaginable livingness" giving birth to every created being, all of

---

20. Stephan Harding, "Towards an Animistic Science of the Earth," in *The Handbook of Contemporary Animism*, ed. Graham Harvey (London: Routledge, 2015), 373.

21. Jorge N. Ferrer and Jacob Holsinger Sherman, *The Participatory Turn: Spirituality, Mysticism, Religious Studies* (Albany: SUNY Press, 2009); Nurit Bird-David, "'Animism' Revisited: Personhood, Environment, and Relational Epistemology," *Current Anthropology* 40, no. S1 (February 1, 1999): S67–91, https://doi.org/10.1086/200061.

22. Gregory Bateson, "Form, Substance and Difference," *ETC: A Review of General Semantics* 72, no. 1 (January 2015): 101.

whom are thus children of a common livingness, is another clue to an animistic interpretation of Wisdom.[23]

Wisdom Christology

There is much debate among Christian theologians about where to "place" Wisdom in relation to the Trinity. Some see Wisdom as the Virgin Mary or another distinct entity; others identify her primarily with Christ; a third group links her to the Holy Spirit, understanding Wisdom as an essential dimension of the love that bonds the Persons of the Trinity and is poured out in creation. Without trying to resolve these debates, I would like to offer the hypothesis of identifying Wisdom first with the "thousands-of-years-old conversation" of all beings with one another, and second with the capacity of Christ to "person" through any of those beings. It would obviously require a much longer discussion—probably several books!—to fully justify such a hypothesis. In lieu of that, I will simply focus in on a few key biblical texts.

After many centuries when most of the focus was on interpreting Christ as Logos or "Word of God," recent decades have heralded the rediscovery of the biblical theologies of Jesus as Wisdom. Scholars have done painstaking scripture study to show how New Testament writers use a wide range of Hebrew Bible texts to interpret Jesus in terms of Wisdom.[24] Several key texts portray Wisdom as a female co-worker with God. In a

---

23. Elizabeth A. Johnson, *She Who Is: The Mystery of God in Feminist Theological Discourse* (New York: Crossroad, 1992), 179.

24. Elisabeth Schüssler Fiorenza, *Jesus: Miriam's Child, Sophia's Prophet: Critical Issues in Feminist Christology* (New York: Continuum, 1994); Elizabeth A. Johnson, *She Who Is: The Mystery of God in Feminist Theological Discourse* (New York: Crossroad, 1992).

long discourse on Wisdom in chapters 8 and 9 of Proverbs, for example, Woman Wisdom stands beside God at the very beginning of creation, assisting God like a master builder (Proverbs 8:30). While these texts are intriguing when applied to the interpretation of Jesus, perhaps even more relevant for the perspective being developed in this book are some of the texts from chapter 7 of the book of Wisdom.

There, as Solomon prays for the gift of wisdom, he declares that it was God who "gave me true knowledge of all that is...[and] taught me the structure of the world and the properties of the elements" (Wis 7:17). He continues, detailing all the instruction about times, seasons, stars, animals, spirits, human beings, plants, and "all that is hidden, all that is plain" that "Wisdom who designed them all" has given him (Wis 7:15–21). Next he describes at length the purity, intelligence, fidelity, and beneficence of Wisdom's spirit, which "pervades and permeates all things" (Wis 7:23–24). Finally, he proclaims:

> She is a reflection of the eternal light,
> untarnished mirror of God's active power,
> image of [God's] goodness....
> In each generation she passes into holy souls,
> she makes them friends of God and prophets. (Wis 7:25–27)

In this text, Wisdom is portrayed as benevolently and actively permeating the design, creation, understanding, and communication of all created beings. There is considerable resonance between this and the way indigenous peoples (e.g., Longboat) describe their participation in an all-beings network of communication and mutual care. Also, the text asserts that it is by being receptive to the communication of Wisdom that human beings can become "friends of God and prophets." As noted in previous chapters, my assumption is that when the Heart at the heart of the world "persons," the resulting epiphany of the heart is not always immediately identified with Jesus of Nazareth. For such an identification, there would have to be a preceding mental context in which it is meaningful. But Wisdom is available to all people, eager to invite them into yoked companionship with the Heart at the heart of the world.

When the gospel writers were searching the Hebrew Bible for help in articulating who Jesus was for their young Christian community, these and other texts about divine Wisdom evidently struck a spark of recognition. Yet how did these authors have a sense of who Jesus was in the first place? One obvious answer, of course, is through the stories about him that had been handed down in the traditions of the communities. These, along with the scriptures, were part of the preceding mental context that they brought to their experiences. Still, these would have produced only barren speculation if the gospel writers and their communities had not been deeply motivated by a personal sense of participation in the ongoing life of Jesus.

It was the experience of Jesus's personal accompaniment, long after his physical death, that gave cogency to the stories of the resurrection and the conviction that he was "the Christ." In fact, the challenge of belief in the resurrection is that it is *only* a participatory truth; every effort to make it objective fails. The early Christian communities, pondering how to articulate who Jesus was for them, recognized him as Christ-Wisdom because they found themselves yoked with him at the heart. As was the case with Peter at Caesarea Philippi, the "rock" of faith is not a monument or even a doctrine, but a living relationship of the heart. Through that relationship of the heart, the first Christians discovered everything that scripture told them that Wisdom would offer them.

Wisdom and the Heart of Mary

It is not surprising that the Proverb texts portraying Woman Wisdom as God's closest co-worker have led to meditations on Mary, mother of Jesus, as an image of Wisdom. Here, we will focus in particular on the connection between this and traditions of devotion to the Heart of Mary.

A common iconography of Christian heart devotion shows the hearts of Jesus and Mary linked together. Such images show his mother Mary as the person who is perfectly yoked interiorly to the heart of Jesus. The most explicit biblical texts referring to Mary's heart include Luke 2:19 and 51, "Mary treasured up all these thing and pondered them in her heart," and Luke 2:35, "This child is destined to be a sign that people will reject, and you too shall be pierced to the heart." Meditation on the Hebrew Bible texts about Woman Wisdom, however, has expanded the view to reflection on Mary's heart as intimate participant in earthly, cosmic, and divine wisdom.

Explicit devotion to the heart of Mary began as early as the twelfth century with Saints Anselm of Canterbury and Bernard of Clairvaux. A number of medieval mystics, including Mechtild of Hackborn, Gertrude the Great, and Bridget of Sweden, wrote of their revelations of Mary's heart. The devotion's more modern form began emerging in seventeenth-century France with Saint Francis de Sales, Cardinal Pierre de Bérulle, and Jean-Jacques Olier. A lengthy treatise entitled *The Admirable Heart of Mary* by Saint John Eudes (1601–1680) brought it to full articulation.

Eudes describes in detail how both Jesus and Mary have "three hearts" (physical, affective, and spiritual) and in each dimension the heart of Mary is perfectly bonded to the heart of Jesus. For Eudes, there can be no more intimate bond than that between the hearts of Mary and Jesus; they are physically, psychologically, and mystically at one with each other. This is the fruit of Mary's *fiat*, "May it be done to me according to your Word" (Luke 1:38). Her radical discipleship of the heart is the ideal model for every Christian. We too are invited to say our own "Yes," yoking ourselves irrevocably in intimacy with Jesus. Only in this way do we too become full participants in the wisdom that is borne within Mary's radical bonding with Jesus.

Significantly, even in the seventeenth century Mary was recognized by Eudes as intimately identified with the Earth. He entitled one of his chapters "Mary's Heart, the Center of the Earth," and wrote:

> It was in Mary, the center of this blessed earth, that God worked out the salvation of mankind. "He hath wrought salvation in the midst of the earth" (Psalm 73:12)....By that is meant the heart and bosom of the spotless Virgin Mary. Yes, it was in the midst of this "good earth," or better, in the good and excellent Heart of Mary, Mother of Jesus Christ, "in a good and perfect heart," (Luke 8:15) that the Eternal Word, coming forth from the Father's bosom to save mankind, was received and zealously nourished, producing fruit a hundredfold and one hundred thousand times a hundredfold.[25]

In making this connection, Eudes was building on earlier traditions that identified Mary with the whole community of earthly life and its spiritual fecundity. Justin Martyr (100–165 CE) and Irenaeus of Lyon (130–202) initiated the tradition of calling Mary "the new Eve" (cf. 1 Cor 15:45, on Jesus as the new Adam) and "the mother of all the living" (Gen 3:20). Bernard of

---

25. Jean Eudes, *The Admirable Heart of Mary* (New York: P.J. Kennedy & Sons, 1948), 42–43.

Clairvaux (1090–1153) wrote that "With good reason is Mary called the center of the earth, for all the inhabitants of Heaven, and those of hell, those who come before us, and those who will come after us, their children's children and their entire posterity look to her as to the midst and the center of the earth."[26]

In Latin America, many indigenous peoples who embraced Christianity have given her the title *Pachamama* (which can be translated as "Mother Earth" or "Earth Mother.") In pre-Christian cultures this was the name of a fertility goddess, so when indigenous Christians use it to identify Mary, they are following the ancient tradition of calling her "the mother of all the living" in a fresh image appropriate to their culture. At the 2019 Synod of the Amazon, this image was used in several of the official prayers and liturgies. Some found this problematic, but Pope Francis and most of the bishops and theologians present accepted it as an appropriate inculturation of ancient teaching about Mary.

Thus both old and new insights recognize in Mary the enfleshed wisdom of the entire Earth community. This wisdom is centered in the radical yoking of her heart with the Heart at the heart of the world. There she found the fountainhead of the physical, affective, and spiritual fecundity that make her "the mother of all the living." There we, too, will find our center of fecundity.

Conclusion

The Heart at the heart of the world resounds in every creature and in the intricate web of all creatures, seeking to communicate Wisdom to us through the fine root hairs of our being that seek their nourishment deep within this web. Jesus, who incarnates

---

26. St. Bernard of Clairvaux, *Serm. 2 in die Pentecost.*

the living dynamism of this mycelial web of Wisdom, invites us to "take up his yoke and learn from him" as we participate wholeheartedly in this visceral flow of life and kinship.

FOR REFLECTION AND PRACTICE:

Whom do you regard as "wisdom figures"? What do you know about how they acquired their wisdom? What is your own way of seeking wisdom?

Reflect on the positive role of imagination in your life. What is the difference between imagination as an "escape" and imagination as creating fresh possibilities for relationship? Play with freeing your imagination as you encounter various creatures of the Earth.

FOR FURTHER READING:

Bruno Barnhart, *The Future of Wisdom: Toward a Rebirth of Sapiential Christianity* (Rhinebeck, NY: Monkfish, 2018).

Steven Chase, *Nature as Spiritual Practice* (Grand Rapids, MI: Eerdmans, 2011).

Robin Wall Kimmerer, *Braiding Sweetgrass: Indigenous Wisdom, Scientific Knowledge, and the Teachings of Plants* (Minneapolis: Milkweed, 2013).

Daniel L. Prechtel et al., *Soul Journeys: Christian Spirituality and Shamanism as Pathways for Wholeness and Understanding* (Berkeley, CA: Apocryphile, 2020).

8

COMMUNITY OF HEARTS

I begin this chapter with some trepidation due to my acute awareness of the disjunction between the idyllic resonance of a title like "community of hearts," and the many pitfalls that commonly plague real-life groups of human beings who attempt to live, work, and/or pray together. I remember so clearly my own first encounters with Christian communities, and how I was swept up into starry-eyed visions of joy and perfect love. I still live rooted in the truth that is revealed in such moments. Fifty-odd years later, however, having spent decades living and working in very dedicated Christian communities, it often requires a daily battle not to give in to a certain cynicism about the potential of humans actually to live the "one heart and one soul" ideal of Acts 4:32.

Bonhoeffer on living in community

Dietrich Bonhoeffer addressed this head-on in his classic text *Life Together*, which he wrote while serving as professor and formation director in a Nazi-era German seminary. Surrounded by the violence and evil of the Nazified culture, Bonhoeffer offered this stark definition of the essence of Christian community life: "Christianity means community through Jesus Christ and in Jesus Christ. No Christian community is more or less than this."[1] It is a great mistake, Bonhoeffer emphasized, to suppose that Christian community life is meant to be the fulfillment of our fantasies of blissful togetherness. If the focus is properly kept on Christ, each person will be humbled first of all by his or her own deficiencies; that, in turn, forms a basis of compassion for the deficiencies of others. He wrote: "Just as surely as God desires to lead us to a knowledge of genuine Christian fellowship, so surely must we be overwhelmed by a great disillusionment with others, with Christians in general, and, if we are fortunate, with ourselves. By sheer grace, God will not permit us to live even for a brief period in a dream world."[2]

Bonhoeffer's emphasis on decentering ourselves through maintaining an explicit, conscious, faith-based focus on Christ works well for groups of humans who identify as Christian. However, in the context of this book we need to explore further what it means to live community based in "the Heart at the heart of the world," whether that is explicitly named as the Heart of Christ or not. Lutheran theologian Lisa E. Dahill has explored how Bonhoeffer's concepts can be extended not only to broader groups of humans but even to the forming of community in an interspecies context. She acknowledges that Bonhoeffer himself, writing in the 1930s and '40s and in a male-only seminary setting, remained anthropocentric as well as androcentric. However, his emphatic insistence that there cannot be one part of reality that is "in" Jesus Christ and

---

1. Dietrich Bonhoeffer, *Life Together*, trans. John W. Doberstein (Princeton, NJ: Harper & Row, 1954), 21.

2. Bonhoeffer, *Life Together*, 27.

another part of reality that is "outside" of Christ means that the application of his core principles cannot be limited to the space within the boundaries of the churches, or even solely to the human species.

Dahill particularly focuses on Bonhoeffer's idea that Christ as divine "other" stands as both boundary and bridge at every encounter of persons. As boundary, Christ protects the integrity and dignity of persons; as bridge, he makes responsible relationship possible. Dahill imaginatively broadens this to the membranes that form the boundaries and bridges within and between all living creatures. These are "those highly generative connective and protective barriers mediating the flows of water, nutrients, energy, waste, and life itself between and among beings—indeed constituting each being—in every pulsing moment of our interwoven lives on Earth."[3] Such encounters in the more-than-human world clearly do not involve conscious relationship with Christ, yet Dahill proposes that they partake of the same dynamic of "person-forming, divine membrane-mediation." Thus, in the very foundations of how life is constructed we can already find the rudiments of the incarnation. Divine life incarnates by bringing forth boundaried beings who are designed to be interdependent with others. Dahill concludes by affirming that the "astonishing mystery of this deepest interior and exterior inter-permeation [is] the gateway to the fullest possible eucharistic life."[4]

3. Lisa E. Dahill, "Rewilding Life Together: Bonhoeffer, Spirituality, and Interspecies Community," *Dialog: A Journal of Theology* 61, no. 2 (2022): 169, https://doi.org/10.1111/dial.12740.

4. Lisa E. Dahill, "The View from *Way* Below: Inter-Species Encounter, Membranes, and the Reality of Christ," *Dialog* 53, no. 3 (September 2014): 256, https://doi.org/10.1111/dial.12122.

Sharing community with other species

This short summary of Dahill's theological work on inter-species community doesn't do full justice to its richness and nuance, but it helps to introduce us to a reflection on the deeper significance of our sharing of life with other species. As a starting point we can recall the discussion in chapter 1 about the microbial community that lives in, on, and around every part of our body. The more scientists learn about this, the more they confirm that it truly is a community in the sense that all resident species are mutually interdependent as they strive together to live their best lives.

The primary example is our gastrointestinal system, which contains a complex ecosystem of 300–500 bacterial species. It has been found that, when in proper balance, these microbes help to sculpt brain and nervous system development, build and maintain the immune system, influence mood and personality, and maintain normal mental health.[5] When microbial balance and relationships in the gut ecosystem become disordered under conditions such as high levels of stress, poor affective relationships, bad diet, infection with pathogens, or exposure to chemicals, these functions are disrupted. The subsequent decline in health may include physical, emotional, and/or mental illness. Autism and schizophrenia are among the conditions that seem to show a strong correlation with disrupted gut ecosystems. Investigation continues into whether these and other illnesses are the cause or the result of problems in the gut; the answer is likely to be some of both, along with many other factors such as genetics and perhaps sheer chance.

---

5. Siri Carpenter, "That Gut Feeling," *APA Monitor on Psychology* 43, no. 8 (September 2012): 50.

What is significant for our purposes, however, is that evidence suggests a mutuality of influence such that damage to any species or relationship in the gut ecosystem has a deleterious effect on the flourishing of the whole communal system.

We may grow to appreciate and nurture this interior interspecies community, but we are probably unlikely to form "relationships of the heart" with microbes. For most of human history, however, humans lived in great intimacy and respect with the exterior ecosystemic communities in which they participated. Hunters by necessity knew all about the habits and preferences of their prey, and farmers were steeped in traditional lore about the intricate labor of nurturing and protecting their crops. Farm animals often lived in the same dwellings as their owners, almost literally as members of the family. Slaughter for meat took place by the hands, and before the eyes, of those who would eat it. While people may or may not have felt affection for the species with which they were interdependent, they had no choice but to viscerally share life with them.

A minority of people, even in a highly urbanized society such as the United States, still live this way. In a 2022 *New York Times* essay, Sarah Smarsh writes about what it was like to grow up as the daughter of a fourth-generation Kansas farmer in the 1980s.[6] She describes how helping her parents to kill and butcher the same cows that she had seen her father midwife into life in cold midnight stables did not desensitize her to reverence for the animals' lives, as this act was just one part of a rhythm of raw interdependence by which both animals and people were bound. When she cut her finger while packaging the butchered meat, she saw that her blood was no different

---

6. Sarah Smarsh, "What Growing Up on a Farm Taught Me About Humility," *The New York Times*, December 22, 2022, sec. Opinion, https://www.nytimes.com/2022/12/21/opinion/farm-meat-butchering.html.

from that of the cow. For her, she writes, "there is no taste of meat without bodily memory—the heat of a newborn calf in my cold arms, the smell of the mother's cascading excrement, the danger of her heavy hooves." Smarsh concludes: "While we lived in poverty, according to many definitions, it was a fortune and privilege to grow up with a big garden, with cows and pigs and chickens."

For most today, that kind of daily intimacy with other species takes place only with our pets, with whom our interdependence is emotional rather than physical. In urban contexts, daily lives are so permeated and shaped by humanly constructed paraphernalia that it takes work for us even to become aware that there is a living ecosystemic community surrounding us. The only time such awareness becomes unavoidable is when a disastrous natural event such as a massive storm, heat wave, earthquake, flood, or fire smashes our constructed defenses and imposes its will on us. A shocking event like this rudely awakens us to how human failure to attend to the dynamics of natural systems can be catastrophic. For example, after a devastating flood we learn that our habits of draining wetlands, replacing native grasses with turf grass, straightening and/or paving watercourses, and filling floodplains with housing developments not only devastate myriads of native wildlife, but also result in awful human suffering. Whether we like it or not, our life and well-being are deeply intertwined with that of the wetlands, watercourses, floodplains, and all the communities of native wildlife that ought to be thriving in them.

Andreas Weber beautifully articulates how the practical, messy, painful, yet beautiful enterprise of community is at the very center of the web of earthly life. He writes: "Life is, at nearly every level, a collective concern, a shared enterprise undertaken by a wide variety of beings that arrive at a stable, functional, and thereby beautiful ecosystem by somehow putting up with one another and reaching agreements."[7] At the heart of every ecosystem, Weber continues, are three fundamental dynamics that constitute the realness of being alive: a longing to be, erotic attachment, and self-giving in death. The longing to be is each creature's innate demand to maintain its wholeness and to grow to its potential. Erotic attachment is the glue of the complex interlinking with a matrix of other beings upon which the survival and fulfillment of each creature depends. Pain and death, finally, are the cost of all this. To be fully alive is to be in a state of transformation fueled by both inner urgency and the play of exchange with others, and "there is no transformation that does not also hurt."[8]

As for death, it is at the center of how nature "sculpts"; "every currently living species exists at the expense of hundreds of others that have long been lost."[9] Thus, in nature death is a form of self-sacrifice—of finally giving over one's being so others can also grow and love. To love, then, "is to welcome death and its mysterious, unending power of transformation and creation."[10] While Weber is not writing from a Christian perspective, it does not require a great leap to make connections between his insights and some basic elements of Christian theology and practice.

Eating, interspecies community, and Eucharist

Everyone has to eat, whether we get our food by hunting and gathering, gardening and farming, or driving to the supermar-

---

7. Andreas Weber, *Matter and Desire: An Erotic Ecology* (White River Junction, VT: Chelsea Green Publishing, 2017), 35.

8. Weber, *Matter and Desire*, 104.

9. Weber, *Matter and Desire*, 149.

10. Weber, *Matter and Desire*, 153.

ket. A reflection on the act of eating concretizes what interspecies community means in today's world. The last thing I ate
before writing this paragraph was a handful of caramel-coated
popcorn. Ingredients include sugar from sugar cane or sugar
beets, butter and cream from cow milk, vanilla from vanilla
plants, and corn. Each of these plants or animals requires specific nutrition and ecological conditions, including the participation of numerous companion microbes, to grow well. Under
current conditions of industrial farming, turning these living
beings into food also requires complex social networks of
human beings who build, sell, and operate agricultural ma-
chines; collect, process, sell and distribute fertilizers; manage
farm operations of planting, tending, and harvesting; transport
by means of trucks, trains, and ships; and, finally, process the
ingredients and package them into the form that I pluck from
the grocery shelf. To function, the body of each one of the thousands of human beings involved depends on both companion
microbes (especially those associated with digestion) and a
wide variety of foods derived ultimately from the death of animals and plants. For me to be able to munch on my afternoon
snack of caramel popcorn, this entire community of multiple
species has had to work together more or less expeditiously.

This is the reality of interspecies community under the
conditions of industrialized food production. However, even
though the coordinated actions of thousands of human beings
and dozens of species (or perhaps tens of thousands, if microbes are fully tabulated) are involved in almost all of our acts
of eating, most of us have little awareness of any of them. Our
only conscious interaction related to obtaining food may be
with the cashier at the supermarket. In *The Meal That Reconnects*, Sacred Heart sister Mary E. McGann details the extreme
destructiveness of the industrial food system that, since the end
of World War II, has nearly eliminated the family farm in favor

of huge industrial farming operations that are cruelly toxic to the health of ecosystems, farm animals, and human laborers alike. This change in the means and type of food production is central to the crises of pollution, climate change, biodiversity loss, and global famine and malnutrition, as well as to escalating rates of diabetes, obesity, social fragmentation, and class conflict. McGann makes the case that getting back to centering food production in small, local, organic enterprises that practice regenerative care of soil and water is essential to rediscovering food as "not a thing but a relationship."[11]

McGann's deeper concern, however, is to demonstrate the link between this more life-giving approach to food production and the Christian Eucharist. During Jesus's years of ministry, he modeled sharing meals with others as a practice of radical generosity and inclusivity. Over and over again we see him welcoming to table fellowship those his culture regarded as outcasts. Even when there does not appear to be enough food for those invited, he insists on inviting—and feeding—even more. For Jesus, sharing food is at the center of forming joyful, just, life-giving communities that are ever eager to draw in wider and more diverse circles of participants. The supper that he shared with his intimate friends on the last night of his life, when he offered his own body and blood as the food that is given for all who hunger and thirst for life, brings this to a climax.

McGann shows how those who follow Jesus, then, are called to revitalize not only explicit eucharistic practice, but all food production and sharing practices. In our explicitly eucharistic assemblies, the bread and wine can be locally grown and prepared. Our Eucharistic Prayers can be rewritten to affirm and celebrate our community with Earth, wild creatures,

---

11. Mary E. McGann, *The Meal That Reconnects: Eucharistic Eating and the Global Food Crisis* (Collegeville, MN: Liturgical Press Academic, 2020), 125.

and the cosmos as well as with the diverse human cultures of the planet. Beyond the sharing of symbolic elements, a full meal can be offered to all—and especially to those most in need of it. These would be first steps toward the truly prophetic praxis of working on behalf of making all food production and sharing as full of joy, justice, inclusivity, and life as the meals Jesus shared with others during his lifetime.

Gift economics

In *Braiding Sweetgrass*, Potawatomi ecologist Robin Wall Kimmerer describes her childhood delight in receiving the land's gift of wild strawberries, extravagantly produced by the nearby wild land each year for free. In the joy of the gift, she not only savored them herself but also loved to pick as many as possible as a gift for her father. Later in the season, she would return and gift the strawberry plants by clearing the soil so their runners could put down more roots. She writes, "Even now, after more than fifty Strawberry Moons, finding a patch of wild strawberries still touches me with a sensation of surprise, a feeling of unworthiness and gratitude for the generosity and kindness that comes with an unexpected gift all wrapped in red and green."[12] Her experience perfectly illustrates the difference between a gift economy and one like our industrial agribusiness systems that are based in extraction of "resources," monetary exchange, and maximizing profit.

All ecosystems are gift economies. Everything is given free, without price; and everything is received the same way. The fox does not pay the mother duck for the ducklings that provide him with his supper; nor do the plants of the forest pay the fox

---

12. Robin Wall Kimmerer, *Braiding Sweetgrass: Indigenous Wisdom, Scientific Knowledge and the Teachings of Plants* (Minneapolis, MN: Milkweed Editions, 2013).

when he drops his feces—and later, his whole body—for their nourishment. The gifts, of course, may be quite expensive; the mother duck loses her offspring, and the ducklings lose their lives. Yet nothing in nature demands reparation—other than that the fox, too, must one day give over his own body for others to eat, without asking anything in return. The cycles of nature operate on the assumption that all will receive what they need and all will give back everything, without the necessity of any explicit system of exchange or barter.

Humans also practiced gift economics for millennia, especially in more face-to-face societies that obtained their food directly from the land. A gift economy is different from an exchange economy in that a person's status is measured by how much they give, rather than by how much they have. In the "potlatch" feast celebrated by many Native American tribes of the Pacific Northwest, for example, the most powerful, honored, and admired person is the one who can freely give an opulent feast and shower expensive gifts on all who come from far and wide. Whereas in an exchange economy the passage of goods from one person to another is impersonal and transactional, in a gift economy the gift creates and nurtures a relationship of joy and gratitude. This awakening of the relational heart overflows the immediate relationship of giver and gifted, making the gifted one eager to participate in further actions of giving. In such a system, even an ordinary person manifests their dignity and honorableness by giving gifts that are extravagant in relation to their means.

Another variation of gift economy is one in which highly valued items constantly circulate, gifted from one person to another without any expectation of immediate recompense. In this case the one who receives the gift must, in due time, give the gift to someone else; if they do not do so, they become social pariahs whom no one trusts. In his book *The Gift*, Lewis Hyde explains how North American colonizers' inability to understand the rules of such an economy of circulating gifts led to the pejorative term "Indian giver."[13] The Native Americans honored their settler guests by offering them valuable ceremonial items as gifts; but when the settlers presumed to keep the gifts as trophies rather than to behave properly by regifting them, the Native Americans were deeply unsettled. The settlers, meanwhile, were equally unsettled by this strange expectation that the gift be "returned."

In my international travels, I have more than once experienced my own variation of this cultural misunderstanding between the instincts of one raised in an exchange economy and those of participants in cultures more oriented to the gift. In the Philippines, for example, negotiations about what I would be paid for my professional services seemed to go in confusing circles until I eventually accepted not being paid at all—which, after all, may be appropriate considering the disparity in wealth between my country and theirs. Yet the director of the program was insistent on taking me on a short holiday tour afterward that included staying overnight in a hotel, and on my departure day I was showered with gifts, some of them quite expensive. I was left feeling a little miffed by not being paid, and at the same time both flummoxed and pleased by the "over the top" gifts. Not having grown up in a gift economy, I lacked an instinctive sense for how to behave in such circumstances.

Eating and being eaten

In February 1985, Australian feminist philosopher Val Plumwood went on holiday for a few days to explore the waterways of Kakadu National Park by canoe. The weather grew ominous

13. Lewis Hyde, *The Gift: How the Creative Spirit Transforms the World*, Third Vintage Books Edition, The Canons 23 (New York: Vintage Books, 2019), 3–4.

but she pressed on in hopes of finding some rock paintings the park ranger had told her about. When she finally turned back, she was startled by a large crocodile who began furiously attacking her canoe. The next thing she knew she was in the animal's jaws, being swept into the "death roll" crocodiles employ to disorient and drown their prey. Plumwood endured three death rolls and several severe bites before she managed to escape and claw her way up the muddy bank of the river. Fortunately, the ranger realized that she had not returned and sent a rescue party during the night; she was taken to the hospital and ultimately survived her injuries without major disabilities. The event, however, became a centerpiece in her future philosophical reflections.

In one of her essays about this experience, Plumwood described how in an instant all her deepest presumptions about herself and her place in the world were thrown into utter disarray. She wrote:

> Before the encounter, it was as if I saw the whole universe as framed by my own narrative, as though the two were joined perfectly and seamlessly together. As my own narrative and the larger story were ripped apart, I glimpsed a shockingly indifferent world in which I had no more significance than any other edible being. The thought, "This can't be happening to me, I'm a human being. I am more than just food!" was one component of my terminal incredulity. It was a shocking reduction, from a complex human being to a mere piece of meat.[14]

Plumwood's reflections do not stop there, however. She observes that in fact all creatures are more than mere food;

---

14. Val Plumwood, "Being Prey," *Kurungabaa: A Journal of Literature, History, and Ideas from the Sea* (blog), January 18, 2011, https://kurungabaa. wordpress.com/2011/01/18/being-prey-by-val-plumwood/.

each one has its own desires, relationships, achievements, and instinctive love of life. Yet we humans have placed ourselves in a separate category, as if we were masters of the chain of reciprocal eating rather than participants in it. The crocodile was not an aberrant monster, even though it felt like one to her. Its assumption that she was food was normal; her assumption that she could not be "just food" was mistaken. Plumwood notes that this mistake in our self-estimation underlies our exceedingly cruel treatment of the animals who are our food; we reduce them to the status of mere food because we are unable to imagine being in their position. Eventually, however, our bodies will indeed be food for some other creatures—despite our use of mortuarial techniques of embalming and sealing corpses in airtight coffins that both delay the decay process and toxify the surrounding soil communities.

In *The Practice of the Wild*, Gary Snyder makes the connection between the modern disconnection from the food chain that Plumwood describes and the suppression of the gift economy that pervades the natural world. He notes that most of humanity prior to recent centuries still "understood the play of the real world, with all its suffering, not in simple terms of 'nature red in tooth and claw' but through the celebration of the gift-exchange quality of our give-and-take." Comparing this to the celebratory character of the Native American potlatch, he continues, "To acknowledge that each of us at the table will eventually be part of the meal is not just being 'realistic.' It is allowing the sacred to enter and accepting the sacramental aspect of our shaky temporary personal being."[15] Snyder, a Buddhist, names what Christians too often fail to see: being food for others is being gift, and that rightly should be called "sacramental."

---

15. Gary Snyder, *The Practice of the Wild: Essays* (San Francisco: North Point Press, 1990), 19.

The gift economy of the Eucharist

The Gospel of John depicts Jesus saying, "Amen, amen I say to you, unless you eat the flesh of the Son of Humanity and drink his blood, you do not have life within you" (John 6:53). Shocked by these words, many of those who had been following him quickly disassociated themselves from him. Their comment, "This saying is hard; who can accept it?" (John 6:60) still applies today. If they thought about it, most people would be shocked and perhaps even disgusted by the idea that in the Eucharist we are eating human flesh and drinking human blood. Generally speaking, those of us who frequent the Christian Eucharist do not think about it this way. The eucharistic ritual comes across to us as a highly compartmentalized and ceremonialized event that is more likely to put us to sleep than to shock us. Since we receive a token of bread and of wine, we recognize the ritual's character as a symbolic meal; but rarely, if ever, do we ponder the implications of Jesus's statement that we must literally "munch"[16] his flesh and drink his blood in order to share in his life.

This shocking reality is worth pondering, however, especially in the context of our previous reflections on nature's gift economy and the role that "eating and being eaten" play in it. The brilliance of Jesus's eucharistic self-giving has many levels, but one we often miss is his complete and unabashed participation in the give-and-take realism of the food network.

---

16. The Greek *trogein* in John 6:54 literally means "gnaw," "crunch," or "munch." James Douglas Grant Dunn and John William Rogerson, *Eerdmans Commentary on the Bible* (Grand Rapids, MI: Eerdmans, 2003), 1179; Jane S. Webster, *Ingesting Jesus: Eating and Drinking in the Gospel of John*, Academia Biblica 6 (Boston: Brill, 2003), 83.

Rather than reacting with horror and avoidance to being reduced to food, he embraces it and makes it into a holy celebration. It is, indeed, like a potlatch where the feast-giver astonishes and delights all those who come to the meal with his over-the-top, even wasteful pouring out of wealth. Or, put another way: Jesus simply accepts, affirms, and finds joy in the world as it actually is—a world in which life requires eating, eating requires death, and no one is exempted from either death or being eaten.

A major challenge in many theologies of the Eucharist is to avoid making it appear as a kind of magical act. When the focus is strongly on the divinity of Jesus, discussion of his act of self-giving in bread and wine often gets mired in complicated debates about "transubstantiation"—that is, how are the physical elements of the Eucharist transformed into something that they were not originally, namely, Jesus's divine-human body and blood? Without disparaging these important theological issues, the approach taken here is to focus first on the humanity of Jesus. As human, he recognizes, accepts, and celebrates the human condition of being among those who must eat and also must be eaten. Moreover, he knows (long before our science and theology were able to spell it out) that to be human flesh is to be implicated in all flesh, that is, in the entire global and cosmic network of the continual exchange of physical components.

Lisa Dahill goes so far as to propose that one of the ways we should understand the resurrection is as the recycling of the decomposed elements of Jesus's body and blood through the food chain and other Earth cycles. The body of Jesus, broken down by the ordinary wear and tear of human life and then even more definitively by torture and death, pours itself out into the Earth and its ongoing cycles of life. Jesus, then, lives again as "a maggot Jesus, a trout Jesus eating the flies born from those maggots, a bear Jesus, a soil and grass and toad Jesus, juniper and cedar Jesus, and countless microbe and bacteria and fungi Jesuses as his molecules dispersed, as they surely longed to do, back into countless new forms of life."[17]

The essential insight is that Jesus's body and his blood are not confined only to the skin boundaries of his first-century human organism. When he blesses and lifts up the bread and wine, infusing the act with all the love of his heart, he reveals and raises up in them what was already true: he participates in them and they participate in him. As we receive them, this participation of heart and body is revealed in us, as well. Without claiming that these insights are sufficient as a complete theology of resurrection and Eucharist, I would propose that deep reflection in this vein is essential to reclaiming Christian mission in an ecological age.

The Australian priest and ecotheologian Denis Edwards asserted, "I believe that in the Eucharist Christians have the source for an authentically ecological ethos and culture."[18] He went on the explore in detail how the eucharistic act expresses and consummates our relationship of kinship with all creatures, as well as how everything that we do in love and care for Earth and its creatures is a continuation of Jesus's eucharistic mission. He concludes: "When the name of Christ is invoked over the bread and wine, the Creator Spirit leads us towards a way of feeling, living and acting as part of a global community of life."[19]

---

17. Lisa Dahill, "Eating and Being Eaten: Interspecies Vulnerability as Eucharist," *Religions (Basel, Switzerland)* 11, no. 4 (2020): 8, https://doi.org/10.3390/rel11040204.

18. Denis Edwards, "Eucharist and Ecology: Keeping Memorial of Creation," *Worship* 82, no. 3 (May 2008): 209.

19. Edwards, "Eucharist and Ecology," 213.

Community with the ancestors

One of the more unfortunate choices made in the history of Christian missions was to suppress the practices of reverent relationship to ancestors that were central in most indigenous cultures. When arriving missionaries saw people practicing rituals such as bowing in front of images, making food offerings, burning herbs or incense, and uttering petitions to the ancestors, they were prone to immediately diagnose this as either idol worship or the deification of human beings. These ancient rituals were forcibly replaced with Christian liturgical practices focused on the triune God. Instead of the ancestors, people were enjoined to venerate Mary and other designated Christian saints. While these do have some things in common with ancestor rites, what is lost is the local, personal, earth-based interconnection that many indigenous people feel with their ancestors. With rare exceptions, the missionaries failed to realize not only how deeply these ancestor veneration rituals were entwined with the very essence of people's cultures, but also what value they have for forming people in essential human, social, and environmental virtues.

Although the specific customs and practices of different indigenous cultures vary considerably, ancestor veneration seems to be a kind of archetypal urge for the human species. Even in modern Western cultures today, it is not uncommon for people to speak of their dead relations as watching over them and having opinions on what is going on. The veneration of ancestors involves the certainty that at least some people live on beyond death, and that our relationship with those who have departed makes a difference in our lives. It provides a foundation for an ethics of making choices for the common good, since in many cultures it is those who have most fully served the good of family and community who receive the honor of being remembered and called upon with the greatest reverence. It inculcates practices of attentive reverence and filial piety in family relations with the living, the dead, and even (in many cases) with more-than-human creation. While the Christian cult of the saints incorporates some of the same concepts, it rarely is able to replace the visceral depth of interconnection with past, present, and future embodied in indigenous relations with ancestors.

In an article on the indigenous cultures of the Belep Islands in New Caledonia and Oʻahu in Hawaiʻi, Emanuela Borgnino and Lara Giordana describe how the planting of a newborn's umbilical cord in the earth connects that child to their ancestors, to that unique place, and to future descendants who will also rise from roots in that earth-place. The infant is already designated as a "future ancestor."[20] The land itself, and especially certain spaces known to be sacred, is inhabited by the invisible presence of spirits and ancestors. To enter those special places, one must be sensitive to, and relate respectfully with, its invisible inhabitants. Only by responsibly observing the proper protocols of behavior in relation to the ancestors can one enter "the flow of life that has been transmitted by the ancestors from one generation to the next and in which the whole life of a person thrives."[21]

To pay attention and to live fully in this respectfulness toward relations visible and invisible, past, present, and future, in this particular environmental place can be quite burdensome —and even more so under today's conditions of severe social

---

20. Emanuela Borgnino and Lara Giordana, "The Disregarded Weight of the Ancestors: Honouring the Complexities and Cultural Subtleties of Islandscape," *Island Studies Journal* 17, no. 2 (2022): 7, https://doi.org/10.24043/isj.403.

21. Borgnino and Giordana, "The Disregarded Weight of the Ancestors," 10.

and environmental threat for indigenous island peoples. Yet this traditional "weight of the ancestors" also has tremendous creative and ecological potential, as it is a constant reminder to attend to and care for one's people and one's place just as they are, in all their vulnerability and precariousness. Borgnino and Giordana conclude that all of us have much to learn from this profound "relational entanglement" that sensitizes these island peoples to, in the words of Donna Haraway, "stay with the trouble" in a time of ecological crisis.[22]

The communion of saints

Some efforts have been made to renovate the Christian doctrine of the communion of saints along ecological lines. In *Friends of God and Prophets*, Elizabeth A. Johnson seeks to shift our understanding of this doctrine away from a patriarchal patronage model, in which the saints have been lifted up to another plane that is distant from us. In that model, our main relationship with the saints is needy supplication so they will intervene with God for us. She argues that a companionship model of the relationship between living and dead is actually more primordial, including among early Christians.[23] As companions, the departed are envisioned as participants in the circle of friendship that is the ongoing community. Like other members of the community, the living dead offer their services to encourage its flourishing. The community returns the favor by venerating

---

22. Borgnino and Giordana, "The Disregarded Weight of the Ancestors," 17; Donna Haraway, *Staying with the Trouble: Making Kin in the Chthulucene* (Durham. NC: Duke University, 2016).

23. Elizabeth A. Johnson, *Friends of God and Prophets: A Feminist Theological Reading of the Communion of Saints* (New York: Continuum, 1998), 79–85.

them. The predominant mood of the relationship is mutual gratitude and delight, rather than distance and neediness.

At the end of her book, Johnson proposes that the companionship model can be expanded to include all creatures.[24] She writes: "The same divine creativity that fuels the vitality of all creation also lights the fire of the saint. The communion of holy people is intrinsically connected to the community of holy creation, and they stand or fall together." In fact, she notes, the Latin term for the communion of saints, *communio sanctorum*, can refer to "holy people" or "holy things." Recognizing the wisdom of the indigenous ancestor traditions, she observes that our modern loss of a sense of tender ongoing relationship with all the beings who have gone before us also cuts off our sense of care and responsibility for those who will come after us. We regard the Earth as relevant only to our own brief life span, rather than as a precious communal heritage to be handed on in the best shape possible.

A parable of family reunion

Robin Wall Kimmerer offers a parable that is a fitting end to this chapter.[25] Every year, she writes, all the species of the Earth hold a family reunion. Everyone comes with a dish to pass and a short speech to inspire the others, and they all have a rollicking good time. The day ends with a great circle dance. For five hundred years, however, the human species has not attended the reunion. Finally, one year they come. The other species no-

---

24. Johnson, *Friends of God and Prophets*, 240–43.

25. Robin Wall Kimmerer, "A Family Reunion Near the End of the World," in *Kinship: Belonging in a World of Relations*, ed. Gavin Van Horn, Robin Wall Kimmerer, and John Hausdoerffer, vol. 1, 5 vols. (Chicago: Center for Humans and Nature, 2021).

tice that the humans don't bring a dish to pass, and they don't seem inclined to wash the dishes, either. However, everyone is glad they finally came. When it comes time for the speeches, though, many of the species can't help but say hard things to the humans, who have done so much damage to everyone. The mood of the party is getting tense.

Finally, Grandmother stands up and shushes the others. With tears in her eyes, she tells the humans that what they all really want to tell them is to please stop forgetting the most basic instructions of the covenant of life. Remember, she says: "We all carry the same spark of life, the same, 'wanting to be,' and our instructions were to care for it, wherever it glows." Reminding the humans that they are the lastborn of all creatures, she continues: "All this time we fed you, provided every single thing that you need, sung you awake in the morning, and sung you to sleep at night, tried to teach you. We have loved you in every way we know how and you didn't even know." Then another leader speaks: "We're asking you to come home. We need you to be good relatives again. Come down off your pyramid and into the circle." Clumsily, the humans finally join the dance.

Conclusion

The parable reminds us of the joy that awaits us when we finally come home again to the community of creatures. But we also hear echoes of the "weight of the ancestors"—the heavy burden that it will be to live faithfully the life of kinship with Earth and ancestors, especially after five hundred years (or more) of wantonness. Everyone who lives with others in family or community knows that it isn't easy. This is why I found myself feeling trepidation as I proposed the theme of "community of the heart." Seeing the joy of community, I may slide toward blithe romanticism; seeing its burdens and failures, I am easily overwhelmed with bitter cynicism. The balance point, though, has to be focusing on the Heart that dwells at the heart of all things, inviting us each day to join the great circle dance of shared life.

FOR REFLECTION AND PRACTICE:

What is your experience of "interspecies community"? Take some time to ponder the different levels of this: microbes in our gastrointestinal system; the animal and plant communities where you live; special relationships you have with specific animals, plants, or places; your awareness of the threatened global ecosystem.

What is it like to ponder literally being "food"? How does this change your relationship to the creatures you eat? How does it give new insight into the Christian Eucharist?

FOR FURTHER READING:

Andrea Bieler and Luise Schottroff, *The Eucharist: Bodies, Bread, and Resurrection* (Minneapolis, MN: Fortress, 2007).
John Hausdoerffer et al., eds., *What Kind of Ancestor Do You Want to Be?* (Chicago: University of Chicago Press, 2021).
Victoria Loorz, *Church of the Wild: How Nature Invites Us into the Sacred* (Minneapolis, MN: Broadleaf, 2021).
Randy Woodley, *Shalom and the Community of Creation: An Indigenous Vision* (Grand Rapids, MI: Eerdmans, 2012).

PART THREE

RE-VISIONING

9

THE ACCOMPANIMENT OF THE PIERCED HEART

On January 20, 2023, the *New York Times* published an article entitled "A Mother's Desperate Fight to Save her Child from Haiti's Gang Wars." It told the story of Mamaille, a Haitian mother of four whose poverty kept the family trapped in a slum where gangs routinely rape, rob, and/or kill anyone who crosses their path. Hearing that a nun named Sister Paesie might be able to help her by taking her beloved daughter to a safe refuge, Mamaille traveled with her daughter to the expected meeting place. Sister Paesie however, was unable to get there because there was too much violence that day. On the way home, the daughter was killed by random gunfire. Then, before she could even arrive home, Mamaille herself was beaten and gang-raped by eight men. She told the reporter, "I would have preferred to die because when you die, it's over, it's finished."[1]

This is a story that pierces the heart. Or at least, it pierced mine. Moved to tears by Mamaille's utter vulnerability, sorrow,

---

1. https://www.nytimes.com/2023/01/20/world/americas/haiti-gang-violence.html.

and despair, I felt a kind of desperate tenderness and compassion for her. My mind railed against all the systems that lay behind her poverty and abandonment. But there was really nothing I could do, other than hold her in my heart and pray for her. From the point of view of the practical world, that looks like "nothing" as well. But is it?

In this chapter, we return to where we began in chapter 1: with the reality of our broken hearts—and the broken heart of creation. The story of the Pierced Heart of Jesus is both an expression of this pervading reality and a divinely compassionate response to it. The above story of my own response to another's sorrow is a starting point for approaching the challenging symbol of the Pierced Heart. A heart that is pierced is no longer whole; practically speaking, it is in a desperate state. On the other hand, it is now open in a new way. It receives and gives in a way it could not before. A new dimension of inter-being[2] becomes available.

Traditions of the Pierced Heart

In Christian heart-devotion, there is no more foundational text than John 19:34–35: "One of the soldiers stabbed his side with a lance, and at once there was a flow of blood and water." The image of the Pierced Heart evokes many meanings and feelings. First, it is an image of a human being dying on a cruel instrument of torture. When the organ of the heart is punctured by a sharp instrument, death follows quickly. This crucified person is like all of us, and indeed like all sentient beings: he is vulnerable to suffering and subject to death. On this level, the image of the Pierced Heart invites us to identification and to

---

2. Thich Nhat Hanh, *Interbeing*, 4th ed. (Berkeley, CA: Parallax Press, 2020).

compassion. We all have our share of sufferings, and we all will die. When we see someone being abused and on the brink of death, we instinctively respond with the desire to console the suffering and, if possible, prevent the death.

By narrowing the primary focus specifically to the heart, the image intensifies the affectivity and depth of our response. The heart as center of love, commitment, courage, integrity, and tenderness draws us in to an awareness of the relationship of our own heart to this person's heart. This is not just any suffering being; it is one with whom our hearts are most deeply bonded. In this context, the piercing of the heart signifies his costly openness. This heart has been opened up for us; it welcomes us completely, even though the price for him is wounding and death. Words attributed to Jesus come to mind. "There is no greater love than this, to lay down one's life for a friend" (John 15:13). Our heart is moved by the sweet joy of love, even in the midst of our sorrow for Jesus's suffering.

The story that accompanies this image says that this person surrenders his life freely. Even while he is being manhandled, tortured, and murdered, he maintains his equanimity and his dignity. Everything about what is happening to him is unjust, yet he does not become cynical, violent, or despairing. The most arresting image of Jesus that I have ever seen is a closeup of Jesus's upper body and face on the cross, his arms spread wide, tears running down his cheeks, and a beatific smile on his face. The image conveys that somehow, the crucified one is embracing this unspeakable horror with love. In all this, Jesus is an inspiring model for us as we negotiate the sufferings and injustices that inevitably intrude upon our lives. We, too, are invited to welcome the whole reality of life, good and bad, with courage, love, and dignity.

But the most evocative detail of all in the story is the statement that "immediately there came out blood and water"

(John 19:35). Some physicians have postulated a physiological explanation: the pressure of hanging by the arms from a cross leads to a buildup of fluid around the heart, and this fluid bursts out along with blood when the lance is thrust into the heart. More important, though, are the symbolic meanings. Water and blood are archetypal images, appearing in cultural and spiritual symbolic expressions throughout the world. Water is especially associated with fullness of life, the slaking of thirst (physical or metaphorical), birth, fertility, purity, and joy. Blood is associated with life, death, suffering, self-giving, kinship, communion, and propitiation for sin. In chapter 2 we explored how the blood and water evoked numerous interconnections with other scripture passages, as well as the weaving of additional meditative, mystical, and doctrinal connections that have been layered on over the centuries.

The outpouring of blood and water from Jesus's heart as he dies on the cross is, if we dare put it this way, the very heart of Christian Heart devotion. Doctrinally, this became the center around which allusions to dozens of other scriptural texts were woven into a theology of the gift of the Spirit, the Church, and the sacraments all being born from the Heart of Christ. It is identified as the central moment of redemption, when Jesus hands himself over to the Father in death and they pour forth the new, purifying life of the Spirit.

Devotionally, it is the moment of the devotee's most intense identification with Jesus's sufferings, inspiring longing to console his sorrow and eagerness to channel the fruits of these sufferings to all in need. In the Alacoque version of devotion to the Sacred Heart that predominated throughout the modern period, this was expressed through the call to participate in acts of penitential reparation. Mystically, the piercing of the heart opens the way to fulfilled intimacy and union when the seeker drinks from Jesus's heart, enters wholly into his heart through the wound, and at the peak may even be invited to exchange hearts with him. From this developed the tradition of nuptial mysticism, which emphasized the supreme delight of union with Christ but always also associated this with concretely sharing in his sufferings.

As we have seen, the richness of symbols, stories, practices, and theological themes that can be (and have been) developed around the Pierced Heart is almost endless. Here, we will focus on a few that seem particularly relevant for our focus on discovering the Heart at the heart of the world.

The mystery of the cross

Meditation on the Pierced Heart puts Jesus's passion and cross at the center of our attention. Celia Deane-Drummond observes that a weakness of Wisdom Christologies can be a tendency to overly emphasize the beauty and harmony of Christ's incarnation as an integral element of creation. When these theologies downplay the cross, she says, they are in danger of becoming "yet another romantic spirituality."[3] A romantic spirituality, in this context, means one whose belief in original innocence paints an unrealistically rosy picture of how the natural world actually works.

Such a view of immanent Wisdom, which as we have seen is based in some parts of the biblical wisdom traditions, needs to be balanced by Paul's comments on wisdom in 1 Corinthians 1:17–2:9. There, referring to the crucifixion, Paul writes, "It was to shame the wise that God chose what is foolish by human reckoning and to shame what is strong that he chose what is weak by human reckoning" (1 Cor 1:27). Christ crucified is the

---

3. Celia Deane-Drummond, *Creation through Wisdom: Theology and the New Biology* (Edinburgh, Scotland: T & T Clark, 2000), 58.

power and wisdom of God, Paul avers, but this is a wisdom that shatters every human attempt to contain it within our systems of thought. If our "wisdom" cannot encompass and transform the truth that the world is full of suffering and death, it is actually a new version of foolishness.

My own confrontation with this came near the end of a thirty-day retreat. Throughout the retreat I was struggling with aspects of my own brokenness that seemed like intractable obstacles to becoming who I longed to be. One morning, as I stood up from my prayer time, I accidentally knocked a glass coaster onto the hard tile floor. The coaster shattered into a thousand small pieces. Cursing under my breath, I quickly went to get a broom and dustpan to clean it up. Upon my return, however, I was stopped short. I saw that the shattered pieces had landed roughly in the shape of a heart! Immediately, the words came into my mind: "Not the broken heart, but the heart that is created in brokenness." This became the central grace of that retreat.

I am still meditating on the meaning of those words which, like a Zen koan, seem to have many depths. The gist of it, though, is clear. Let go of your angst about the brokenness, real as it is; God is already making something new in the very midst of the brokenness! This is the wisdom of the cross, compassionately holding the broken heart and yet mysteriously re-creating it at the same time.

Trauma: devastation and gift

Still, the reality of brokenness has to be honored before it can be let go. The technical term that psychologists use to talk about deep inner brokenness is "trauma." Trauma occurs when a shocking event radically overwhelms a person's ability to maintain a basic sense of control, coherence, and trust. The well-known trauma theorist Judith Herman wrote, "At the moment of trauma, the victim is rendered helpless by overwhelming force."[4] Those who are seriously traumatized feel as if the very core of their being has been invaded and shattered. Extreme or repeated trauma, such as serial sexual or physical abuse or long-term exposure to unpredictable violence, may lead to deep numbing or, even worse, to the dissociation of parts of the self. The deeply traumatized person no longer feels even a minimal level of safety, wholeness, trust, or ability to cope. Symptoms of traumatic reaction may vary considerably, but common ones include anxiety, relationship problems, depression, and agitated or violent responses to what would ordinarily be manageable challenges.

Psychologists emphasize, however, that the core of trauma is not actually the event, no matter how horrific. Trauma is the person's reaction to the event. Some of those who experience a terrifying event—say, a catastrophic hurricane, a mass shooting, or even a sexual assault—may be deeply shaken, yet recover fairly quickly without major lasting effects, while others may experience long-term incapacitation due to their traumatic reactions. Many factors play into the different responses, but psychologists suggest that the most important factor seems to be how the person has experienced being lovingly accompanied, both before and after the event. It is when the person feels isolated and radically unsafe that the disintegrating effects of painful or shocking events embed in body and soul, literally changing the structure of fundamental neural networks.[5]

---

4. Judith Lewis Herman, *Trauma and Recovery*, rev. ed. (New York: Basic Books, 1997), 33.

5. Bonnie Badenoch, *The Heart of Trauma: Healing the Embodied Brain in the Context of Relationships*, A Norton Professional Book (New York: W. W. Norton & Company, 2018).

Most discussions of trauma understand it as a psychological effect of identifiable historical atrocities, whether these were visited upon individuals or groups. Some, however, view trauma as a more universal human condition that is foundational for our spiritual lives. Stanislav Grof and Binnie A. Dansby are among those who have built practices on the conviction that the experience of birth itself causes profound trauma, especially under the conditions of the modern world where in most cases the very first experience of newborns is to be separated from their parents and subjected to various impersonal tests and other indignities. They teach that re-experiencing and releasing the birth trauma is essential to regaining one's birthright of vital energy and spiritual wholeness.

Going even further, some write of a "sacred wound" that is cosmic in nature, and in which all living beings participate. Richard Rudd describes the origin of the sacred wound as the fracture of the Big Bang, when the utter quiescence of the divine breaks forth into time and space. Life comes forth with an urgency to heal the cosmic wound, and it can do so only by a winding, eons-long path to reunion with the silence and infinite peace of the divine. The wound is sacred, Rudd says, because "it is an integral part of existence."[6] Without it, we would not have within us the dynamism that moves us to face all the challenges involved in pursuing our spiritual growth and ultimate fulfillment.

The philosophy and spiritual practices that Rudd proposes to come to terms with this cosmic "sacred wound" that is built into our very existence are quite complex, and they appear to be more in line with ancient Gnostic teaching than with Chris-

---

6. Richard Rudd, "Hologenesis and the Sacred Wound—the Story behind Your Profile," *Gene Keys* (blog), n.d., https://genekeys.com/articles/hologenesis-and-the-sacred-wound-the-story-behind-your-profile/.

tian theology. Nonetheless, his concept of the sacred wound converges in some important ways with that of Franciscan priest Richard Rohr. Rohr meditates on the fact that Jesus's cross is the gateway to radical renewal and reconciliation. He writes, "The huge surprise of the Christian revelation is that the place of the wound is the place of the greatest gift."[7] It is through our struggles with our own wounds that we learn to let our overflowing pain be transformed into outflowing love. Christianity, says Rohr, is "the way of the wound."

The basic concept of the sacred wound is that, for human beings, being wounded is not only unavoidable but, ultimately, it is given to us as a precious path to wholeness and holiness. In fact, it is not only "a" path but "the" path—there is no other way to becoming who we are created to be than by enduring the crucible of coming to terms with our many-layered woundedness. Without being wounded, a person does not feel an urgency toward the kind of deep personal change that is truly healing. We will not seek reunion with the deepest ground of our own being unless we truly feel the agony inflicted on ourselves and others by our separation from it. The heart must know its brokenness before it can allow itself to be recreated. This may be one of the meanings of Jesus's words, "Take up your cross and follow me" (Mark 8:34; Matt 10:38 and 16:24; Luke 14:27). To find the fullness of life, we must follow the one whose wounds are imaged as openings from which the waters of everlasting life flow.

We must take note here that despite the deep wisdom enshrined in these teachings about the sacred wound, they can be misused. They do not provide an excuse for condoning sufferings imposed on other people, or for a simplistic assumption

---

7. Richard Rohr, "The Sacred Wound," Center for Action and Contemplation, October 16, 2015, https://cac.org/the-sacred-wound-2015-10-16/.

that "pain is good for you." Some wounds are so profoundly destructive that finding the inner resources even to survive becomes heroic. The wisdom of the teaching of the sacred wound is that our wounds can be goads to doing the inner work necessary to open ourselves to moving from the broken heart to the new heart that is created in brokenness. This work cannot be forced on someone who is not ready, however. The best we can do is to offer the gift of accompaniment.

The power of human accompaniment

Psychological research indicates that people whose infancy and early childhood were marked by deep affective responsiveness on the part of their caregivers have much more inbuilt resilience in the face of potentially traumatic events. Their neural networks have been shaped by preverbal memories of tenderness and empathy, and they can fall back on these when they are confronted by shocks such as failure, betrayal, or violence. For all people, however, regardless of their early experience, compassionate accompaniment after the horrifying event makes a tremendous difference in its long-term effects. While there is no way to avoid the intense physical and emotional pain that preoccupy a person in the immediate aftermath of such an experience, a milieu of warm acceptance and understanding can help to prevent it from becoming neurally encoded in way that will seriously impede future functioning.

Post-traumatic stress disorder (PTSD) is what happens when the shattering memory does get neurally embedded in a way that repeatedly triggers dysfunction. The best therapy for a deeply embedded traumatic memory is to bring it to light again in the presence of one or more safe, compassionate listeners. When the trauma is severe, this usually requires the help of professionally trained listeners over a period of months or years. In this way, psychologists say, the neural flashpoint of memory that has been causing so much terror and dysfunction can be gradually reprogrammed so that instead of triggering panic, it is surrounded by an awareness of acceptance and safety.

The most obvious form of healing accompaniment, and the one psychologists usually focus on most, is human accompaniment. For someone to feel deeply accompanied, though, it requires more than the simple physical presence of other human beings. Even someone paying close attention and sincerely trying to help may not be enough. Psychologist Bonnie Badenoch distinguishes between two styles of being "helpfully" with another person. The style that has more commonly been taught in the training of psychotherapists is to focus on "interventions" or techniques that the helper can offer. She recommends, instead, that the foundation of therapy should be simply embracing the other person with warm, unconditional acceptance.[8]

Badenoch grounds this distinction in the work of Iain McGilchrist, who has revived and expanded the insight that the right and left hemispheres of the brain project very different experiences of the world.[9] While the left hemisphere is busy analyzing the world and figuring out how to get things done by linear processes, the right hemisphere relies on intuition and affect to perceive the world holistically. Badenoch's argument is that psychologists who rely too much on calculated interventions prepared by the left brain end up being ineffective. The heart of healing accompaniment, she asserts, is to cultivate the right brain's capacity for warm, intuitive, non-judgmental presence. The psychologist does not need to know "what to do"

8. Badenoch, *The Heart of Trauma*.

9. Iain McGilchrist, *The Master and His Emissary: The Divided Brain and the Making of the Western World*, new expanded ed. (New Haven: Yale University Press, 2019).

for the person, because the deeply accompanied person will discover the inner wisdom to figure that out for him or herself.

This is very similar to what aspiring spiritual directors are generally taught. Most spiritual directors do not have professional training in psychology; their official role is not to assist in the healing of psychological wounds but to accompany spiritual growth. In practice, the distinction is not always that clear. The real difference is that in spiritual accompaniment the presence and guidance of God is explicitly affirmed and invited as the primary agent of growth. Badenoch's reliance on the "inner wisdom" of the person can be seen as a nod in this direction, without using religious language. The actual practice of the spiritual director is strikingly similar to what Badenoch proposed for her psychologists: the cultivation of warm, intuitive, non-judgmental presence, and reliance primarily on what this allows to arise in the one being accompanied.

More-than-human and divine accompaniment

There is another kind of accompaniment, however, that is only now beginning to be given its due: the accompaniment of the more-than-human world. Recall that in the introduction I quoted Sarah Elton's definition: "More-than-human refers to contexts in which multiple species and processes come together to produce a result."[10] That is an abstract way of saying that we humans are never in human-only environments, but rather are always in the company of a whole host of interacting species and beings who support us and, perhaps, at times hassle

---

10. Sarah Elton, "More-than-Human," in *Showing Theory to Know Theory: Understanding Social Science Concepts through Illustrative Vignettes*, ed. Patricia Ballamingie and David Szanto, vol. 1 (Ottawa, ON: Showing Theory Press, 2022), https://ecampusontario.pressbooks.pub/showingtheory/chapter/more-than-human/.

us as we go about in the world doing our business. That humans find relaxation, relief from stress, and spiritual inspiration by spending time attending to more-than-human landscapes and relationships is not new. Accounts describing such refreshing sojourns in nature can be found in the literature of every era and culture. What is new is the scientific research that backs up the insight that both mental and physical health are far more dependent upon our more-than-human relationships than we have generally acknowledged.[11]

In chapter 6 I introduced the practice of Forest Therapy, whose motto is "The Forest is the therapist; the guide opens the doors." The premise of Forest Therapy is that anyone can be guided toward awakening to awareness of deep relationality with the creatures and features of the natural world, and that this is a healing experience. The guide offers invitations, but it is up to each participant to discover specifically how the natural world is calling her or him, at that moment and in that place, to awaken to relationship. Most participants find themselves entering into a slowed-down, receptive, liminal state in which the world sparkles with freshness and delight. It is, perhaps, what McGilchrist would identify as the intuitive, all-at-once, relational perception in which the right brain specializes. The sense of joyful accompaniment within the web of the more-than-human world is intense, and is indeed healing.

Recently I had a prayer experience that opened this up more fully for me. I was meditating on Matthew 12:13, in which Jesus encountered a man with a withered hand on the Sabbath. "Stretch out your hand," Jesus said, and when the

---

11. Mark Payne and Elias Delphinus, "A Review of the Current Evidence for the Health Benefits Derived from Forest Bathing," *The International Journal of Health, Wellness, and Society* 9, no. 1 (2018): 19–30, https://doi.org/10.18848/2156-8960/CGP/v09i01/19-30.

man did so, his hand was healed. This is typically read as a demonstration of Jesus's extraordinary divine power, intervening forcefully in the natural order to bring about miraculous healing. On that day, however, my meditation took me to a very different awareness. I felt myself stretching out the wounded and withered places in myself, opening them with trust to the tender welcome of the web of life and the cloud of ancestors who always have and always will surround me. Jesus was not separate from that, but in it—in each being and in the whole community and in every act of care. He is, and has been from the beginning of creation, the community-making Heart that fuels all beings with the love, dignity, and courage to be with and for one another. I felt deeply healed, as if a withered part of myself was newly filled with life and potential to take up my place in that web of care.

This was a very personal meditation, and I make no claim that it is an adequate exegesis of the text. It is, however, both the genesis and the fruit of the insight that I am developing here. It is the discovery that we exist always and everywhere within a milieu of interbeing that breathes with the life and love of God. Moreover, the Pierced Heart symbolizes that in a powerful and fresh manner.

The pierced heart is an open heart. Rather than being autonomous and whole unto itself, the heart is opened so that what is within flows out and what is outside finds a way to enter in. In the case of the heart as a physical organ, this wounding is fatal—and the image of the Pierced Heart acknowledges that. In other dimensions of the heart, however, it has a different meaning. The pouring out and the welcoming in become constitutive of this Heart. Insofar as this is the Heart of God, it is an image of divinity as living in the very midst of the pouring out and welcoming in that constitutes life and its relationships. Divinity is the Heart of that flow of interbeing; like a heart, its rhythms power, enliven, and purify each and all of the flowing relationships of the web of life.

Luke B. Higgins is saying something similar, I think, when he writes about "intensive alliance" as a foundational metaphor.[12]

> I offer the phrase intensive alliance as a new organizing metaphor for theological cosmology.... Heaven is to be sought precisely in and through the dynamic, intensive flows of earthly becoming.... [Divinity is] that which inspires and enlivens all entities in the cosmos in their complex, intensive relationships of mutual becoming. This conception of the divine can open the way to a truly transformative eco-theology in which God's call is heard in and through our immediate interactions with our living ecology.

Higgins's term "intensive alliance" is abstract, though evocative. He is trying to name the passionate, wholly given way in which the divine is involved with everything that happens in creation. Using my terminology of "the Heart at the heart of the world" brings this back to being concrete, personal, and relational. The image and story of the Pierced Heart go yet further, identifying this way of being with Jesus and the whole biblical tradition. Yet at whichever of these three levels one claims this perspective, the last part of the quote from Higgins is key. We know and participate in the love of God *in* accompanying and being accompanied within the web of created beings, not separately from that.

---

12. Luke B. Higgins, "Energy, Ecology, and Intensive Alliance: Bringing Earth Back to Heaven," in *Cosmology, Ecology, and the Energy of God*, ed. Donna Bowman and Clayton Crockett, 1st ed. (New York: Fordham University Press, 2012), 126–27.

Ecological trauma and mourning

In our time, we are experiencing an epidemic of what might be called "creational trauma." Essentially all ecosystems are being subjected to destructive shocks from which fewer and fewer of them have the capacity to recover. In her essay "A Threat to Holocene Resurgence Is a Threat to Livability," Anna Tsing proposes that the difference between previous ecological disturbances and those occurring today is that there are fewer and fewer *refugia*.[13] A *refugia* is an intact ecosystem to which threatened animals and humans can relocate, and it is also a place where living animal, plant, and fungal members of the ecosystem can survive so that damaged ecosystems can draw from them later on to re-establish themselves. This is, of course, a considerably oversimplified account, since ecosystems have always been in motion, extinctions have always been occurring (though at a vastly slower pace than today), and no ecosystem ever returns to an exact copy of its former patterns. What Tsing is pointing to, however, is that the renewal of life after destruction that was possible in previous epochs is becoming increasingly impossible in the Anthropocene.

Perhaps we can discover a loose analogy between the healing potential of ecosystemic *refugia* and our earlier discussion of compassionate accompaniment after human trauma. The analogical dimensions are relationality and safety. All beings, including human persons, thrive when feeling safe within a strong and healthy web of relations. Just as a person whose inner ecology has been shattered seeks the safety of embracing,

---

13. Anna Lowenhaupt Tsing, "A Threat to Holocene Resurgence Is a Threat to Livability," in *The Anthropology of Sustainability*, Palgrave Studies in Anthropology of Sustainability (New York: Palgrave Macmillan US, 2017), 54, https://doi.org/10.1057/978-1-137-56636-2_3.

unconditionally accepting presences, whether human or more-than-human, so the members of a fatally degraded ecosystem are in search of a refuge providing food, shelter, and safety where they can reconstitute their relations. After devastation, the patterns of life may never return to exactly what they were before the trauma; but a new life can be woven if one finds a place to thrive within a refreshed web of relations.

Despite heroic efforts of ecological conservation and restoration in some locales, the tragic reality is that the trend around the globe is toward widespread, rapidly escalating ecological degradation. Nearly all of us experience this locally, for example in weather changes, the steep decline of bird and insect species, and the increase in habitats taken over by invasive species. Ask almost anyone and you will hear a story about the disappearance or degradation of their favorite wild getaway spots. Even more troubling are bigger trends such as plastic and chemical pollution even in the depths of the ocean and the blood of newborns, the destruction of coral reefs and rain forests, and the rapid melting of polar caps. How can we provide *refugia* on such a massive scale? Clearly, as individuals or even by joining with small groups of activists, we cannot. Often, our instinctive response to this looming catastrophe is to hide from it.

Doug Burton-Christie has written about how crucial it is, both for ourselves and for the future health of life on our planet, that we consciously reclaim the practice of mourning for our kin in the web of life. We naturally mourn when our kin—someone to whom we are closely related—suffers or dies. When we hide from the suffering and death of our ecosystemic kin, what we are really hiding from is our own vulnerability within the web of relations that constitutes us. Burton-Christie writes:

> The ability to mourn for the loss of other species is . . . an expression of our sense of participation in and responsibility

for the whole fabric of life of which we are a part. Understood in this way, grief and mourning can be seen not simply as an expression of private and personal loss, but as part of a restorative spiritual practice that can rekindle an awareness of the bonds that connect all life-forms to one another and to the larger ecological whole.[14]

For help in relearning how to mourn, Burton-Christie calls upon the ancient desert tradition of *penthos* (Greek for compunction) and the accompanying gift of tears. The desert monks wrote about tears as a painful, frightening, yet also joyful awakening of an intense awareness of intimacy and kinship with God and all beings. For them, to be flooded with tears was the premier sign that one had fully embraced one's fragility, sinfulness, and need for God's grace, and that one was finally ready to be deeply transformed. The monks used the phrase "the piercing of the heart" to describe this.[15] The tears of a pierced heart signal one's brokenness—one's awareness of being overwhelmed by "the tear in the fabric of the whole"[16]—and thus are a prerequisite to openness to being reknit into a new communion in which God is the primary reality and all beings are one's kin.

The refuge of the pierced heart

Availability to having one's heart pierced by the damage and death being wrought upon the Earth, then, is an essential

---

14. Douglas Burton-Christie, "The Gift of Tears: Loss, Mourning and the Work of Ecological Restoration," *Worldviews: Global Religions, Culture, and Ecology* 15, no. 1 (2011): 30, https://doi.org/10.1163/156853511X553787.

15. Irénée Hausherr, *Penthos: The Doctrine of Compunction in the Christian East*, Cistercian Studies Series, no. 53 (Kalamazoo, MI: Cistercian Publications, 1982).

16. Burton-Christie, "The Gift of Tears," 34.

ecospiritual practice for our time. It will not be easy. In a review of a book on the contradiction between the practice of slavery and the ideals of freedom being proclaimed at the time of the American Revolution, Jon Meacham notes that most of the founders knew slavery was wrong, but concluded it would be too inconvenient to their own interests to give it up.[17] In our own era, most of us are caught in a similar dilemma in regard to the extractive, exploitative, and polluting practices that are razing ecosystems and fueling mass extinctions. Realizing that they are wrong is a first step, but the extreme inconvenience of resisting them stops us in our tracks.

Perhaps the practice of opening our hearts to be pierced is exactly what is most needed at such a moment. The pierced heart does not claim to be righteous or to have all the answers to the dilemma that confronts us. Rather, it cries out in the agony of knowing its fragility and its participation in evil; it recognizes its impotence and its absolute need for grace. At the same time, the heart breaks open to be a place of refuge for all its human and more-than-human kin whose lives are being violently diminished and extinguished. Holding them in refuge means bearing them within one's heart, calling upon all the powers of heaven and Earth to protect and heal them. It means weeping with and for them, helpless and yet fiercely committed to accompany them to the end.

Yet perhaps at such a moment we hear the words of James 2:15–16 coming to unsettle us: "If a brother or sister is poorly clothed and lacking in daily food, and one of you says to them, 'Go in peace, be warmed and filled,' without giving them the things needed for the body, what good is that?" Calling upon

---

17. Jon Meacham, "Can the Country Come to Terms with Its Original Sin?" https://www.nytimes.com/2023/01/17/books/review/american-inheritance-edward-larson.html.

all the powers of heaven and Earth for help means also remembering that we, too, are one small node in the interwoven net of those powers. What does it really mean to become a refuge? What does all this mean, on a practical level? These are some of the questions we bring into our final chapter.

FOR REFLECTION AND PRACTICE:

Go to a nearby park and spend a couple of hours wandering around, experiencing accompanying and being accompanied by the creatures you encounter there.

We hear every day about people around the world who are in horrifying situations because of war, climate change, natural disaster, or fraud. Ponder: How are our hearts pierced by their sorrow? How can we offer these wounded ones the gift of accompaniment, even from afar?

FOR FURTHER READING:

Bonnie Badenoch, *The Heart of Trauma: Healing the Embodied Brain in the Context of Relationships* (New York: W. W. Norton, 2018).

Denis Edwards, *Deep Incarnation: God's Redemptive Suffering with Creatures* (Maryknoll, NY: Orbis Books, 2019).

Solnit, Rebecca, *A Paradise Built in Hell: The Extraordinary Communities That Arise in Disaster* (New York: Penguin, 2010).

10

REPARATION IN THE KEY OF ACCOMPANIMENT

In our time, many thinkers are making sweeping proposals for how the next phase of human life on Earth should proceed. There is a general acknowledgement that the Earth has entered a new geological epoch, primarily characterized by the utterly ubiquitous impact of human activity on every aspect of its functioning. The Holocene—an 11,650-year-long epoch of "mild and constant climate that enabled civilization to flourish"—has ended. Even if humans disappear, says Clive Hamilton, this gentle climate will not return.[1] While the most common name for the emerging epoch is the Anthropocene, we are choosing instead to call it the Ecozoic. It was Thomas Berry who coined this title to emphasize the necessity of the next phase of human life on planet Earth being one of collaboration with the entire community of Earth creatures, rather than a continuation of the exploitative mentality of recent centuries.

---

1. Clive Hamilton, *Defiant Earth: The Fate of Humans in the Anthropocene* (Cambridge, UK: Polity, 2017), 4.

Regardless of the name given it, however, the transition to this new epoch will be arduous and full of both predictable and unpredictable dangers. Among the theories for how to proceed through the difficult period that lies ahead are posthumanism, ecomodernism, and the "new anthropocentrism." Each tells a different story.

Perspectives on the Anthropocene

The most common approach of those who are fully cognizant of how bad things are is posthumanism. Posthumanists assert that modernity, along with its accompanying myth that we humans can take charge of our destiny and move forward in never-ending "progress," is over. Faced with the massive damage that our arrogant ways have wrought upon our ecosystemic habitats and communities, we must accept that we are not the masters and dominators of nature that we imagined. Rather, humans are just one more species, no more "in charge" than the microbes or the weather—either of which is quite capable of sending us to extinction just as we have sent so many others. The Earth is not fundamentally benevolent or communitarian; rather, it is volatile, chaotic, and ruthless. Already deposed from our throne and cast face-first into the trash-heap we have created, our only choice is to muddle along, attempting as best we can to negotiate with all the other powers of the Earth in hopes that a few members of our species may be granted a minimalist survival.

While posthumanism tends to be dourly pessimistic, ecomodernism takes the opposite tack. It is essentially the optimistic assertion that the ecological breakdown we are witnessing in our time is a painful phase on the way to something even better than what existed before. Typically, it includes the additional assumption that new technologies will soon enable us to remedy existing ecological damage and re-engineer Earth systems to maintain or even increase our comfort level. For example, in the face of rising global temperatures, climate manipulation by geoengineering tricks such as seeding the ocean with iron or shooting huge amounts of silver iodide into the atmosphere is being seriously discussed. Most scientists, however, think that the side effects (many of which are unpredictable) of such massive interventions would be likely to make the remedy more damaging than the disease—a classic case of doubling down on the behavior that has caused the problem in the first place. The fundamental assumption of this type of ecomodernism is that deep change of human mentality is not really needed, because the problems we face can be solved by better and more sophisticated application of the same technological means that we are already using. In short, it continues to endorse the modernist "myth of progress" even as the foundations crumble out from under it.

There is another variant of ecomodernism that is more spiritual—and perhaps more familiar to readers of this book. This is the idea that humanity as a whole is on the verge of making a breakthrough to a new level of consciousness or spiritual maturity that will change our attitudes and behaviors so as to resolve existing damage and usher in a new era of global harmony. Many of those who embrace this viewpoint draw on the work of Pierre Teilhard de Chardin, who wrote of the universe's ineluctable movement toward Omega Point (Christ) and the emergence on Earth of the noosphere—the unified mental and spiritual process of humanity, operating at a higher level of complexity than the geosphere and biosphere. This view is termed ecomodernist both because it constitutively embraces the modern myth of progress, and because it often considers advanced technology as a potential ally in the coming shift to a harmonized and humanized Earth. This more spiritual approach does call for deep inner change on the part of human beings, and proponents often strive to offer guidance for how to help this change take place. However, the optimism of believing that such radical change will happen quickly enough, or on a large enough scale, to turn around the ocean liner of human history before it hits the iceberg of ecological collapse seems to lack a certain realism.

The "new anthropocentrism" is a third approach that tries to mediate between posthumanism and ecomodernism. Here the argument is that the human species is indeed different from, and in certain ways more powerful than, all other species. Nonetheless, our current dilemma arises because we have terribly misconstrued our actual character as a species. Clive Hamilton writes: "The original fault in the growth-driven techno-industrial system is its *monstrous* anthropocentrism rather than its anthropocentrism as such. The problem is not that humans are anthropocentric, but that *we are not anthropocentric enough.*"[2] His point is that if we really knew ourselves, we would recognize that while we have never been equipped with autonomous freedom to dominate the Earth, we do have the capability and the responsibility to change it. Our amazing capabilities, however, are necessarily constrained by their factual embeddedness in the processes of nature.[3] At this point in the history of our species, we have created our own worst adversary by unifying the entire Earth system to fight ferociously against our world-dominating ambitions. Only when we accept both the greatness and the smallness of our abilities will we be able to take up, with appropriate humility and restraint, both our power and our responsibility within the total Earth system.

---

2. Hamilton, *Defiant Earth*, 43.

3. Hamilton, *Defiant Earth*, 51.

Pessimism and hope

The view I am developing in this book draws something from each of those presented above. With the posthumanists, I am more impressed with the humbleness of human ability than with its greatness. I believe that nothing is more needed at this point in human history than our acceptance that we are just one among many interdependent species, not born to be masters or dominators. And my reading of what scientists are telling us about the next couple of centuries suggests that they are likely to be horrific, with massive extinctions, terrifying weather and disease phenomena on an increasingly regular basis, and the chaotic collapse of many human populations. On that level, I think pessimism is realism.

With the "new anthropocentrists," though, I affirm human responsibility in this time of crisis. The embrace of post-humanist pessimism too often leads to despair, or to an "eat, drink, and be merry, for tomorrow we die" mentality. Instead, we must stand up and do what we can. With the eco-modernists—and especially those of the "spiritual" version—I believe that humans are capable of so much more than we have yet manifested. The center of this profound capability, however, is not that of physical power, intellect, or technological expertise. Rather, it is our ability to live "heartfully." The challenge is that for most of us, it takes even more commitment, discipline, and time to develop this capability than the others mentioned. It is difficult, therefore, to foresee it happening quickly or on a mass scale.

It takes a long time to learn that pessimism is not the same as hopelessness, and hope is not the same as optimism. Optimism places belief in an upbeat outcome—usually one whose contours one has already defined in one's expectations. Hope, on the other hand, trusts that goodness constitutes the true heart of reality, even when one cannot see how or where this goodness may manifest itself. Hope does not predict whether one will live or die, or whether there will be a happy ending in any foreseeable future. It only affirms that goodness exists, that one can choose it, and that doing so will make all the difference.

A simple story told years ago by one of my former students illustrates hope. He had been imprisoned in harsh conditions by an authoritarian regime. He did not know whether he would ever be released, or whether he might even be killed. In prayer, he realized that he could choose the joy of living. He chose to take delight in the air, the water, the scraps of food, and the companionship of fellow prisoners. His life was changed. Joy became his predominant mood, even while suffering continued.

The story shows what it means to live heartfully. Aligned with the Heart of his God in prayer, this young man discovered the capacity of his own heart to choose love and connection even in the very midst of a death-dealing reality. He was not rescued from the vulnerability of being wounded by abuse, hunger, and anxiety. Instead, he learned the visceral truth of the words of the Song of Songs 6:8: "Love is strong as death.... Love no flood can quench, no torrents drown." There is hope, because there is a Heart at the heart of the world.

Re-visioning the Sacred Heart

We need new visions of how to live in this unprecedented moment in human history, when everything is at stake. The traditional devotion to the Sacred Heart had roots in scripture and theological reflection, but its popularity and effectiveness were fueled by the literally visionary experiences of several medieval mystics and, later, Marguerite Marie Alacoque. In Alacoque's visions Christ revealed to her how his Heart was wounded by human indifference and blasphemy, and he called for very specific acts by devotees to show him the appropriate love. With the help of her Jesuit advisors, this was developed into a theology of reparation that understood the honor of God, offended by juridical sins, as requiring reparation in the form of penitential suffering by devotees. We might call this "reparation in the key of penance." It had a heyday of popularity, but in the twentieth and twenty-first centuries this mentality has made less and less sense to people.

Visions like those of the mystics do not arrive on command. However, we can also think about vision in the broader sense, as when we say of someone that "she has a powerful vision for how we can move forward." We usually don't mean by this that the person has had a mystical vision; rather, we mean that she communicates a way forward that we find inspiring, wise, deeply rooted, and attractive. Visions of either kind (mystical or otherwise) come from a deeper source than the rational mind. A person whom we regard as a visionary leader is one who speaks with conviction from the heart. Normally, of course, this is reinforced by their ability to marshal reality-based facts and theories in order to enflesh the vision. The rational mind is partner to the heart-based vision, rather than the other way around.

If we return to Marguerite Marie's original visions, before their later theological development in concert with her Jesuit advisors, it is clear that they are centered on a nuptial relationship of love with Jesus. She saw that Jesus is wounded by not being loved, and that he wants to show Marguerite Marie exactly what she (and others) can do to love him. The elements of divine honor, the horror of sin, and the need for penitential suffering are not emphasized to the degree that they would be later in the promulgated theology of reparation. In recent reinterpretations of Alacoque's life and work, Benoît Guédas, rector of the Sanctuary at Paray-le-Monial, develops the claim that her core message of the healing love of God was sound.[4]

Yet in view of all the insights presented in this book, there remains a need for re-visioning in view of the specific crisis of our time. Today, the message of the Sacred Heart is that the Heart at the heart of the world is indeed being grievously wounded, but not so much by the failure of humans to perform proper juridical acts of reverence as by our failure to be humble, responsible participants in the web of life on Earth. The Heart at the heart of the world passionately wants to ignite the flame of love in our hearts so that we might live in the abundant flow of divine love, participating in healing the wounded and creating conditions in which all life can thrive.

A new vision requires sorting out what kind of story meets the need of this moment of crisis. In the introduction, I reviewed Arthur Frank's work on the different types of stories generated by people who are facing life-threatening illness.[5] First to arise is the naming story—"What is this? What is happening to me?" Next, often, is the restitution narrative: "This is going to get fixed. Everything is soon going to return to normal." But always looming just around the corner is the chaos narrative of breakdown, panic, uncontrollable suffering, and death. Frank proposes that what is needed in such a moment is, instead, a quest narrative. This is a story of the process of illness as an arduous adventure on the way to personal integrity and wisdom. In such a story, the expectation is that one will

---

4. Benoît Guédas, *Le réveil de la miséricorde: l'appel du Sacré-Coeur de Jésus à Paray-Le-Monial* (Paris: Éditions Emmanuel, 2015); Benoît Guédas, *Dans Le Coeur de Jésus: Sainte Marguerite-Marie, Maîtresse de Vie Spirituelle* (Emmanuel, 2022).

5. Arthur W. Frank, *The Wounded Storyteller: Body, Illness, and Ethics* (Chicago: University of Chicago Press, 1997).

face unimaginable challenges, that one will suffer, and that one will not be the same at the end. The purpose of the quest may be fulfilled even if one dies on the way. The chaotic elements are not eliminated, but heartfully embraced.

The quest narrative, as presented by Frank, remains individualistic. This is not surprising, since the subjects of his research were individuals dealing with serious illnesses. What we are examining in this book, however, is an illness of the entire Earth system, including both its human and more-than-human components. The story told by Marguerite Marie's visions also envisioned a radical and catastrophic "illness" understood in terms of the damage caused by human sin, but it was presented as only a matter between humans and an autocratic God who had been offended. She offered a kind of spiritual restitution narrative: if humans perform the correct devotional actions, God will repair all the damage. Our situation today, however, calls instead for a communal quest narrative—a story of an arduous journey in search of how to be human, with wisdom and integrity, in humble and healthy relationship with the whole community of God's beloved creatures.

The Heart on the cross

At the center of any story of the Sacred Heart is John 19:34, the account of a lance thrust into the heart of Jesus on the cross and bringing forth a flow of blood and water. A strong tendency in Christian theology has been to tell the story of the cross in terms that are both death-focused and triumphalistic; that is, Jesus's violent death is required by God and highly to be celebrated, but once it has happened, death is immediately and unequivocally swallowed up by life. The implications of such a way of telling the story can include a glorification of voluntary suffering along with a dismissal of the ineradicable impact of involuntary suffering on individuals and communities, human and more-than-human. The theology of reparation that developed in the Alacoque tradition of the Sacred Heart followed in this pattern. It contributed to the stream of *spiritualité victimale* or "victim spirituality" that became deeply embedded in Catholic spirituality, encouraging devout people (especially women) to impose pain on themselves as well as discouraging them from resisting suffering imposed by others (for example, domestic abuse).[6]

In her book *Spirit and Trauma: A Theology of Remaining*, Shelly Rambo proposes a different way of telling the story of the cross and what flows from it. She starts with a review of some of Hans Urs von Balthasar's writings in which he stressed the central importance of the "Holy Saturday" period between Jesus's death on the cross and the stories of his resurrection. Using as one of his key sources the mystical visions of his close associate Adrienne von Speyr, Balthasar rejected the traditional triumphalistic view that Jesus descended to hell only to conquer it and bring its denizens back with him to heaven. Instead, Jesus truly went to hell, completely abandoned by his Father. In his poetic reflection *Heart of the World*, Balthasar describes the Holy Saturday period this way: "There is nothing more but nothingness itself. The world is dead. Love is dead. God is dead. Everything that was, is a dream dreamt by no one. The present is all past. The future is nothing. The hand has disappeared from the clock's face."[7]

---

6. Giuseppe Manzoni, "Victimale (Spiritualité)," in *Dictionnaire de Spiritualité Ascétique et Mystique, Doctrine et Histoire*, vol. 17 (Paris: G. Beauschesne, 1932), 531–45.

7. Hans Urs von Balthasar, *Heart of the World*, trans. Erasmo S. Leiva (San Francisco: Ignatius Press, 1979), 150.

Rambo is fascinated by how Balthasar depicts this sheer chaos that ensues upon Jesus's violent death. She recognizes it as comparable to the experience of trauma survivors, who find themselves trapped in vicious cycles of chaos. Rather than replacing the chaos quickly with a "restitution narrative" of triumphant resurrection, Balthasar describes a witness lost in darkness. Only gradually does the witness begin to glimpse obscure flashes of light and a tentative awareness of something oozing, a "chaotic drop" that is too thick to be water and too colorless to be blood. Balthasar then writes: "Slowly, slowly, unbelievably slowly the drop begins to quicken.... It trickles, lost in the chaos, directionless, without gravity. But more copiously now. A wellspring in the chaos."[8]

Rambo focuses in on this witness in the chaotic darkness as a true depiction of what it is like to be a trauma survivor. After the violent shattering of one's world by trauma, there is no return to the world as it was before. An ineradicable agony has been planted in the center of one's being. Yet something persists; gradually, the survivor discovers that they are obscurely accompanied in the darkness. Rambo finds a similar pattern in the Johannine stories about Mary Magdalene's encounters with Jesus after his death. Mary Magdalene, she says, "points to a different kind of presence, whose form cannot be readily identified or can only be received through multiple experiences of misrecognitions. She encounters not simply the absence of Jesus, but a mixed terrain of his absence and presence. He is there but not there; he is present in a way that she has not known before."[9] Despite the confusion of this "mixed terrain," Mary Magdalene knows that something has been

---

8. Balthasar, *Heart of the World*, 151.

9. Shelly Rambo, *Spirit and Trauma: A Theology of Remaining* (Louisville, KY: Westminster John Knox Press, 2010), 91.

handed over to her; she becomes a witness to Jesus's love that persists and accompanies, even in the ongoing obscurity.

This chastened theology of the cross is appropriate for our era of global and planetary trauma. Rather than celebrating death, this theology faces the ineradicability of its shattering reality. It does not offer a story of quick or complete healing from the devastation of trauma. It affirms the confusion and darkness within which we must make choices about how to go on after devastation. Yet, within all this, it offers the obscure yet certain conviction that someone is here with us, silently sharing with us the courage and love to persist amidst the ruins. There is a Heart at the heart of the world, even when most of what we are able to see and feel is death.

Reparation in the key of accompaniment

In her book *The Love of Nature and the End of the World*, psychoanalyst and environmental philosopher Shierry Weber Nicholsen explores why it is that so many of us who know that the damage our way of life is doing to the world may be fatal for our species (not to mention its devastating impact on thousands of other species) nonetheless keep silent, avert our eyes, and go on as if nothing were happening. Her writing is rich and poignant as she takes a clear-eyed look at the psychology of our paralysis in the face of this escalating "chaos narrative."

In her final chapter, Nicholsen develops the concept of the "holding environment" as what is most needed in order to face and survive the global trauma in which we are all immersed. This concept comes from the work of another psychoanalyst, D. W. Winnicott, who described how infants need to be held both physically and psychologically in a manner that combines safety with freedom. Held in this way, the child can experience ruptures of relationship (initiated by either partner) and can also begin to gain the skills needed to repair these ruptures.

The concept has subsequently been extended beyond infancy; persons at each stage of life need a stage-appropriate "holding environment" in order to be free and courageous enough to risk the pain and failure that are inevitably involved in any exploration toward growth. Nicholsen's answer, then, to the question "What should we do?" is this:

> We should create holding environments, and use the ones that already exist, to reflect on the issues of our relationship to the natural world and its deterioration. We should do so by exercising leadership, from whatever position we occupy, using the sources of support available to us, and with as much thoughtfulness and self-awareness, courage, and generosity as we can muster.[10]

This paragraph provides a key to what might be called "reparation in the key of accompaniment." Whereas the traditional understanding of reparation focused on penitential suffering in order to make up for the dishonor suffered by God, this approach focuses on heartful forms of relationship that free human and more-than-human creatures to discover their own creative way toward repaired relationships and conditions of thriving. In what follows, I offer several examples of proposals for creating "holding environments" that awaken the heartful potential of the human and more-than-human world.

The heart of an educator

"The heart of an educator" is a phrase that is frequently used in my own religious congregation, the Society of the Sacred Heart. The congregation was founded in the aftermath of the French

---

10. Shierry Weber Nicholsen, *The Love of Nature and the End of the World: The Unspoken Dimensions of Environmental Concern* (Cambridge, MA: MIT Press, 2003), 197.

Revolution, which was a deeply traumatizing time for Catholics. Churches were being vandalized, then closed and repurposed; religious congregations were violently disbanded; and nuns and priests were forced to abandon their vows and sometimes were even killed. In the context of this moral and ecclesial devastation, Madeleine Sophie Barat (1779–1865) had a vision of a world re-ordered around the Sacred Heart and the self-giving love of the Eucharist. Inspired to see that the way to enflesh this vision was through the education of girls, she began founding schools. Today, there are schools of the Sacred Heart on every continent—160 schools in all, with some for boys as well as girls.

Janet Erskine Stuart, a British Society of the Sacred Heart leader of the early twentieth century, wrote that there are two approaches to forming strong, competent people of good moral and spiritual character. The direct method teaches very clear guidelines and rules for how a person should behave and do their duty. The indirect method, however, "is longer and less clearly defined. It aims at giving a guiding light within, and power to climb a difficult path, and pick a way through unknown country by that light. This must be waited for, and slowly developed, but in the end it is of greater worth."[11] She concluded that the latter is the aim of Sacred Heart education. What Stuart calls the "indirect method" requires the educator to recognize that a heart able to accompany another person with wise, faithful love is more effective than any specific content or technique of education.

This vision of Sacred Heart education has also broken open to be enfleshed in many other forms besides schools. Whether with children or adults, whether in schools or in any other context, heartful presence is more foundational than whatever else one may offer. It is this presence that enlivens the

---

11. https://www.sacredheartusc.education/mission/founding-mothers/ janet-erskine-stuart/quotes-by-janet-erskine-stuart.

heart of the other and awakens them to become their best self, not only intellectually but also emotionally and morally. Accompanied people discover the inner resources of courage, confidence, openness, generosity, and vision that enable them to enflesh love in the world in practical ways. This is the line that Saint Madeleine Sophie Barat drew from the Sacred Heart to the repair of a fractured society.

Ecological restoration as mutual accompaniment

In the previous chapter we looked briefly at how the accompaniment of the more-than-human world can play an important role in the healing of trauma. Here we will look at a concrete practice through which humans and ecosystems can mutually accompany one another toward increased vitality and integrity.

In *The Sunflower Forest: Ecological Restoration and the New Communion with Nature*, William R. Jordan III describes three concepts of the human relationship with nature. First, the colonialist concept understands nature as something to manage for human benefit, enhancing its value for recreation, hunting, or "ecosystem services" such as clean water or oxygen. Second, the concept of nature as sacred place recognizes a landscape's intrinsic value and, on that basis, strives to protect it from human intervention. Finally, the concept of nature as a community in which humans participate recognizes that there has always been, and always will be, an ongoing mutual interaction between humans and the landscapes where they are present. The goal, then, is to develop this interaction into patterns that are genuinely mutually beneficial. Jordan develops the third concept in terms of the practice of ecological restoration.

Ecological restoration is a scientific practice of working in concert with a degraded landscape to promote conditions in which it can restore itself to health. While often the hope is that the landscape will come closer to resembling what it was in the past, the reality is that no past condition can ever be fully re-created. In the U.S. Midwest region, for example, tallgrass prairies covered 167 million acres, hosted millions of bison, and existed largely undisturbed from the end of the last Ice Age until about two hundred years ago. With less than 4 percent of the original prairies remaining, numerous restoration projects are under way. Most, however, involve a few hundred or at most a few thousand acres, and it will take decades or longer for them to sustainably approximate the biodiversity of the original ecosystem.

Jordan makes the case that under current conditions of breakdown affecting both humans and the more-than-human world, widespread active participation in ecological restoration projects is the best hope for both. Many humans today find ourselves either with practically no interaction with the more-than-human world, or with a consumerist, romanticized relationship in which we use nature for occasional pleasant experiences and forget about it the rest of the time. The activity of restoration is a physical way to get personally engaged in knowing and caring about a specific local ecosystem. It can be compared to creating a mutual "holding environment" in which the restorer and the ecosystem hold one another in a way that enables each to thrive.

Jordan compares participation in ecological restoration to a kind of alchemy, as it involves "a self-transforming attempt to return a piece of land to some earlier condition, not outside history but independent of the restorationist, and therefore outside his ego."[12] This work is also a kind of play. With hands in the dirt, attending to the slow pace and complex interac-

---

12. William Jordan, *The Sunflower Forest: Ecological Restoration and the New Communion with Nature* (Berkeley, CA: University of California Press, 2003), 78.

tions of natural change, one makes friends with local creatures and is humbled by one's relative lack of power in this community. Restoration, says Jordan, is a process of experimentation and learning that proceeds as much, if not more, through failure as through success. It brings ecology back to its roots as a healing art.[13]

Ritual, community, and sacrifice

As an act of building community with the more-than-human world, restoration work also calls forth the creation of rituals. Ritual is how communities admit members, manage boundaries, and deal with ambiguous dimensions of relationships. We need to ritualize our commitment to, and delight in, our partnership with the more-than-human world. However, we also need to come to terms with the ways in which life in this community unavoidably involves ambiguity or even shame. Within the work of ecological restoration, the ambiguity is that favoring a return to better biodiversity and balance in an ecosystem almost always requires killing some of the living beings that currently exist there. A common example is the culling of overly abundant deer whose feeding habits are destroying too many native plants. Often there is an outcry against this practice by those who feel bonded with the deer. On an even more fundamental level, the chief ambiguity of life in the community of all Earth creatures is that members of this community inevitably impinge upon and even destroy one another in the process of meeting bodily needs. Our discussion of "eating and being eaten" in chapter 8 reflects on this.

As Nathaniel F. Barrett puts it, moving into the future as an ecological community of humans and other species will

---

13. Jordan, *The Sunflower Forest*, 81.

require "the wider development of a new kind of emotional competency...for engaging in a difficult but also deeply rewarding form of participatory ecological community."[14] Rituals that symbolize and work through the reality that sacrifice and death are unavoidably part of the fabric of life in this community will be essential in building this emotional competency. As an example, Barrett proposes that before burning a prairie (an action that will kill many fragile beings, but in the longer term promotes the health of the prairie ecosystem), restorers engage in a ritual dramatizing the beauty as well as the destructive power of fire and acknowledging the sacrifice about to be made by the beings who will die for the sake of the community's well-being.

One source for developing such rituals is study of indigenous practices. Many indigenous communities who lived in close contact with predators and also practiced the predatory activity of hunting ritualized their relationships with these animals, recognizing their dignity and agency as well as asking their cooperation and forgiveness. Another source is our own biblical and Christian liturgical traditions. As we saw in chapter 8, the liturgy of the Eucharist resonates with ancient themes of coming to terms with violence, death, and sacrifice in the context of forging the bonds of community. We also have liturgies of reconciliation and forgiveness, and rich textual traditions celebrating the divine presence in the more-than-human world. We might paraphrase Matthew 13:52 and say that the disciple of the kindom of God has treasures both old and new to weave together to foster the life of this multispecies community.

---

14. Nathaniel F. Barrett, "The Promise and Peril of Ecological Restoration: Why Ritual Can Make a Difference," *American Journal of Theology and Philosophy* 32, no. 2 (2011): 155.

Practicing paradise

We all long to live in paradise. Traditionally, paradise has been envisioned either as an original Eden, lost through sin, or as a future heaven, attainable only by the grace of God after passing through death. In an essay entitled "Practicing Paradise: Contemplative Awareness and Ecological Renewal,"[15] Doug Christie explores the ancient Christian tradition that paradise is simply our present world welcomed in its deepest reality. Everything in the created world is both gift of God and redeemed in Christ; all that is lacking is for us to open the eyes of our hearts to recognize this beauty and wholeness. Two realities, however, stand in our way. One is the all-too-evident brokenness of the world. Violence and evil mar the world's beauty with a horrifying ugliness from which we dare not turn our eyes, lest we fall into romantic escapism. The other problematic reality is our own anxiety. This has many sources, but at root it rises from the ego's belief that it must save itself by its own fragile achievements.

In the tradition of the desert monks, Christie observes, to live in the contemplative simplicity of paradise was to live free from care; it was to live "purposelessly." The ego-blinded mind that reduces everything to its utility cannot see or relate to anything simply as it is. As anyone who practices prayer can attest, the greatest mistake we can make (and one that we all make over and over again) is to try to "achieve" something in our prayer. Contemplation, says Christie, "has no end or purpose beyond itself. The contemplative seeks only to become more

---

15. Douglas E. Christie, "Practicing Paradise: Contemplative Awareness and Ecological Renewal," *Anglican Theological Review* 94, no. 2 (2012): 281–303.

aware of, more alive to everything and everyone." Paradoxi-
cally, this practice of contemplative purposelessness actually
does have "a *telos* or end toward which it moves and which it
helps to facilitate: the great consummation or recapitulation of
all things in God, the new heaven and new earth long dreamed
of by prophets and mystics."[16] This *telos* is fulfilled, however,
only by surrendering to the sheer grace of the Heart at the
heart of the world.

Christie proposes that in the current global reality of catastrophic ecological degradation, "practicing paradise" is a necessary starting point for healing the world. We practice
paradise when we open our hearts to accompany and be in
community with the web of life that surrounds us, just as it is.
This is not a practice to be done only in beautiful, relatively
pristine places that effectively seduce us with their loveliness.
Rather, it is to be done anywhere, unveiling the beauty and
God-given wholeness that are the deepest reality even in landscapes where ugliness is what more obviously meets the eye.

In chapter 6 we learned about the emerging theology of
"deep incarnation"—the insight that Jesus's bodily participation in the cycles of air, water, and soil through the natural
functions of his human body means that the incarnation is not
only into a single body but into the total Earth system.
Christie's proposal could be called "deep resurrection," as he
calls us to "risk inhabiting and embodying in our own lives the
truth that the whole world has risen in Christ."[17] To practice
paradise is to trust wholeheartedly in the Heart at the heart of
the world. Only thus will we find the love, courage, and confidence to do whatever else must be done.

16. Christie, "Practicing Paradise," 296.
17. Christie, "Practicing Paradise," 303.

Conclusion

I conclude with a story that exemplifies both the risk and the joy of practicing that level of trust in the midst of a world in danger. The story is told by David Abram, who while paddling his kayak along a rocky Alaskan shore suddenly found himself confronted by dozens of agitated, roaring sea lions, each of which weighed as much as twenty-five hundred pounds.[18] Instantly realizing that he could not paddle fast enough to escape, he followed his first instinct and began to half-howl, half-sing back to them. This seemed to calm them until, just at the wrong moment, a humpback whale violently breeched between Abram and the sea lion colony, riling them all up again into attack mode.

Abram writes: "I do not know by what wisdom, or folly, my animal organism chooses what to do next. Of course, there are not many options, and no time to think: my awareness can only look on in bewilderment as my arms fly up over my head and I begin, in the kayak, to dance." Amazingly, this once again calmed the animals. By tuning in to them at this bodily, rhythmic level, Abram established a relationship with the sea lions. Instead of continuing to react to him as a threat, they tentatively began to accept his friendly accompaniment and sharing of life. It still required some expert paddling—while still dancing—to get away to a safe distance. His life had been saved, however, by the act of viscerally entrusting himself to the wisdom of the "Great Conversation."

Few of us will face an angry colony of sea lions, but all of us face the dangers of an Earth that is increasingly restive due

18. David Abram, *Becoming Animal: An Earthly Cosmology* (New York: Vintage Books, 2010), 159–66.

to the unwise provocations of humans. We can learn from Abram's experience that the best way to save our lives—and those of future generations—is by finding a way to accompany the agitated creaturely world, entering as friends into its rhythms of song and dance. This is what it means to "practice paradise" in the Ecozoic era.

FOR REFLECTION AND PRACTICE:

Sign up to volunteer for a few hours with a group that is engaged in restoration work in a park or nature refuge near your home. Journal about your experience.

Play with developing a personal ritual for reconciliation with the natural world around you. Examples could be praying to the four directions; hugging a tree; creating a circle and sitting with the creatures who enter or pass by. There are infinite possibilities—use your own creativity!

FOR FURTHER READING:

Diana Beresford-Kroeger, *To Speak for the Trees: My Life's Journey from Ancient Celtic Wisdom to a Healing Vision of the Forest* (New York: Random House, 2019).

Douglas E. Christie, *The Blue Sapphire of the Mind: Notes for a Contemplative Ecology* (New York: Oxford University Press, 2013).

Margaret Swedish, *Living Beyond the "End of the World": A Spirituality of Hope* (Maryknoll, NY: Orbis Books, 2008).

INDEX

heart
  brokenness of, xiii–xiv, xvi, 4, 6, 182,
    186, 189–90, 198
  as center of devotion, 16
  as center of love, 14, 183
  cosmic, xxii, 14
  dimensions, 7–8
  divine, 13, 32, 77, 79–80, 109, 135
  and dualism, 10
  heartfulness, 8
  interpretations of, xii, 4–5, 23–25
  physical, 3–4, 13, 24, 30, 32
  pierced, 182–85, 194–95, 198–99,
    207
  spiritual, 13, 32
  yoking of, 133, 136, 154
heartbreak, xvii, xix, 199
Heart Devotion, 29–30, 38, 40
heart-experience, 7, 12–13, 19
heartfulness, 8–9, 19–20, 69, 134
heartlessness, xi–xii, xxii, 30
Heart of Christ. *See* Sacred Heart of
  Jesus
Heart of God, xxii–xxiii, 30–31, 36–37,
  80, 82, 84, 88–90, 119, 132, 147,
  194
Heart of Mary, 33, 152–53
Heart of Matter, The (Teilhard), 36
Heart of the World (Balthasar), 210
heart qualities, 69, 79, 85
Herman, Judith, 187
heteronormativity, 101, 103, 109
heterosexuality, 101–3
Heyward, Carter, 106
Higgins, Luke B., 195
holding environment, 212–13, 216
Holocene, xiv, 50, 53, 78, 201
Holy Spirit, 28, 32, 121, 130, 146, 149
Holy Trinity, 66
homo sapiens, 72, 77–78, 81, 86–87
homosexuality, 100–102, 107
How Forests Think (Kohn), 125
Huff, Barry, 95
humanism, 30
humility, 31, 60, 66, 132, 146, 204
humus, 59–60
Hyde, Lewis, 166

illness, xvii–xviii, xxi, 11, 159, 208–9
  mental, 140, 159
Incarnate Word, 31–32, 39
incarnation, 68, 88, 119, 123, 146, 158,
  220
inculturation, 15, 154
indigenous cultures
  and animism, 54–56, 123
  appropriation of, xxv
  and interconnection, 137, 142, 150,
    173
  and missionaries, 15, 173
  and Mother Earth, 49, 154
  and shamanism, 139–41
Ingerman, Sandra, 143
Ingold, Tim, 118
interconnectedness, 10, 95, 109, 118–19,
  137–38, 173–74, 184
interdependence, 6, 49, 62, 117, 142,
  160–61
interiority, 5, 7, 12, 16, 68, 88, 121, 133–
  35, 144
intersex, 105–6
interspecies community, 157, 159–60,
  162–63
intersubjectivity, 134–35
Irenaeus of Lyon, 24, 153

Jeanne de Chantal, 31
Jennings, Theodore, 107
Jesus Christ
  and androcentrism, 105
  and chaos narrative, 210–11
  and ecomodernism, 203
  and Eucharist, 170–71
  and Mary, 152–53
  as new Adam, 25, 153
  as new Moses, 146
  and nuptial mysticism, 185
  and Paneas, 113–17
  and personhood, 118–20, 126, 128–
    30
  pierced heart, 24–28, 182–84, 193–
    95, 207, 209
  preexistence of, 66–67, 73–74, 88–89
  and sexuality, 105–9
  three hearts, 13–14, 32, 152